PAYING PROJECTS FOR CLUBS

Paying Projects

FOR

Clubs

Tested and Practical Suggestions for Fund-raising
by AILEEN MALLORY
Associate Editor, Capper's Farmer

Publishers

T. S. DENISON & COMPANY

Minneapolis

Dedicated to my club-going relatives,
loyal members of worthy organizations

Dear Club Friends:

When I was writing Club Notes for CAPPER'S FARMER, many women wrote, "Tell us how we can make money!" With that plea in mind, I have collected material for this book.

Included here are long-time favorites. If your group hasn't tried them, they will be new to you. I have also introduced some new projects, many of them experimental. Perhaps they will challenge your members.

Every idea is a suggestion only. Adapt it to suit your situation. Or let it stimulate new, and possibly better, ideas.

There is bound to be some overlapping of subject matter. If you don't find what you want in one chapter, look in another.

I sincerely hope you will find something here helpful for your club. May your projects pay off — in making money, sharing work, and having fun.

Good luck!

AILEEN MALLORY

CONTENTS

INTRODUCTION

Did you know the average woman belongs to three women's clubs? There isn't much doubt that at least one of those clubs needs a money-making project sometime.

How you raise money depends on several things peculiar to your club.

1. Your motives. Why are you trying to make money? Is it for the good of the club itself, for a worthy cause, or just to keep up with the Jones Club?

2. Economic conditions. Can the majority of your members actually afford to donate? Perhaps they can occasionally, but don't ask too often.

3. Age and experience. Young members may suggest a big project with enthusiasm, only to hear older members groan. Try to balance the fund-raisers so everybody gets a chance to do something she likes, or can do. Don't expect the elderly to take as active a part as young women.

4. Outside help. Avoid working husbands, local merchants, and outsiders too much. They'll probably all do their part—within reason. But don't ask for cooperation repeatedly.

5. The size of the project. This can be determined by the cause. If you simply want funds for a little social club, don't expect the whole community to join in. If your organization is of interest to the whole town, or you're sponsoring a worthwhile charity, throw a big affair. Give everybody a chance to help or to buy a ticket.

Only the bigger clubs can swing the elaborate shows. So the number of members you have in your club, their ability and willingness, are probably the deciding factors on the size of your project.

Chapter One

SALES FOR MEMBERS ONLY

Sometimes many small money-making projects at club meetings during the year can bring in almost as much money as one elaborate public project. Those members-only sales can be highly entertaining, too. You might like to try a few on your group.

What to Sell at Club Meetings

Yard Auction

Announce that at the next meeting each member is to bring a yard of something, tied up in a paper bag. Maybe you'd better set a price range. Bags are auctioned off, sight unseen. Some of the things that a bidder is liable to get are: a yard of safety pins, a yard of plastic, a yard of hot dogs, etc. This sale is really fun.

Pint Auction

This is a variation of the sale given above. In this case, members bring a pint of something. Better set a minimum value so no one shows up with a pint of water!

Black Cat Auction

 This is a new name for the usual white elephant auction. It is based on the idea that it is unlucky to have unused, unwanted articles about the house. Have members bring their castoffs and sell them. It's surprising how much someone else will pay for something one woman simply cannot stand!

Who's Who?

Ask members to list their name, address, telephone number, birthdate, and hobby. Collect these and have them compiled into an alphabetical list. To make it more helpful, add a blank page for listing additional phone numbers and addresses. Sell this mailing list at slightly above the cost of printing or mimeographing. Especially good just before the Christmas card mailing season!

Hateful Housework

Each member lists her most hated household task. She also writes down the price she'll pay to have it done. Example: "$3.00 to iron Ed's dress shirts for one week;" "$1.00 to scrub my kitchen floor once;" "50c to frost the next cake I bake," etc. You'll be surprised how one woman's "hate" will be grabbed up by another. She is allowed to keep half of what she earns doing the "hate," but must turn the other half into the club treasury.

Apron Strings

The women serving the refreshments make, or buy, inexpensive aprons to wear. These are sold to the highest bidder when the serving is finished. One catch—the buyer may have to launder her purchase before she can wear it!

It's in the Bag

Each member is asked to donate some kind—any kind—of bag. You may get laundry bags, sewing bags, shopping bags, clothespin bags, maybe even paper sacks!! These are all auctioned off! To carry out the theme, serve refreshments in a paper bag.

Sweet Profit

Ask members to bring bottles of cologne, perfume, bath salts, etc., that they don't want. (Probably you have received such gifts. You either didn't particularly like the fragrance, or were overstocked.) Remove labels and put on price tags. Members sniff and buy.

Hi-lo Auction

Each brings a wrapped package. On the outside she writes the highest price she thinks it is worth and also the minimum she thinks the article should bring. Then the auctioneer will know about when he should let the item go, or if he should hold it longer for a higher bid.

Mrs. Easter Bunny Sale

Ask a few women who aren't too busy to dye some eggs. It might be a good idea if they are farm women as they will probably have plenty of eggs. Then auction them off at the meeting nearest Easter. Mothers of young children may be delighted to get eggs dyed this easy way!

Old Hat Sale

Each member brings an old hat in a paper bag. They are auctioned off, unopened. Each must wear the hat she buys while she eats her lunch. This is lots of fun, even though each hat brings only a small amount of money.

May Baskets

At your May meeting, sell May baskets filled with home-made candy.

Valuable Time

Sell slips of papers listing every minute in an hour. (For example: 2:01, 2:02, etc.) Members pay a penny for each minute they buy, with no limit on amount they can purchase. Place several alarm clocks around the room. Each is set to go off at a different time but within the designated hour. (Example: 2:13, 2:21, etc.) Persons who "bought" the minutes the alarm sounds, get an inexpensive prize.

Pattern Exchange

Members bring patterns that are in outgrown sizes or for which they have no further use. Sell these at below cost They should be smart basic styles, in good condition. If the outer envelope is missing so the buyer cannot see what the pattern looks like, sell it as a Mystery Style. These should sell a little cheaper than a pattern with a descriptive picture.

Second Look Books

This is merely a new name for a sale of second-hand books. Be sure they are in good shape and no pages missing. If any comic books are donated, it is a good idea to "censor" them.

Rags to Riches

Ask members to bring clean rags to a meeting. Sort and sack these and sell them to local print shops, garages, etc.

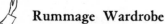

How to Sell at Club Meetings

Rummage Wardrobe

If you're planning a rummage sale at a meeting, ask the women to wear at least one outworn garment they plan to donate for the sale. It adds to the fun and starts the sale off with a bang!

Backward Auction

This sale works in reverse! The longer you wait, the cheaper the article gets. For example: A loaf of homemade bread might start at 25 cents, and finally end up at five cents. Don't worry— no one can bear to see something sell too cheap; especially the women who made it! She'll probably buy it back before she'll let it go at a loss.

Good Riddance Bingo

This combines entertainment with money-making. Prizes for Bingo are unwanted articles brought to the meeting by the members. If a player doesn't like her prize, she then holds a quick auction. If, at the end of the game, there are still some items left, box them for a charitable institution.

Sing-Along Auction

Each member brings a "white elephant." She wraps it and writes on the outside the name of a song that she thinks describes the article inside! "In the good old summertime" might be on a fan from the attic. "Take me out to the ball game" could be a baseball or catcher's mitt. This one is entertaining because it combines guessing with buying. When a woman is high bidder, she tries to guess what is inside by the song given. If she guesses it, she can open it. If not, she must pay one more penny!

That's the Ticket!

Sell tickets at a penny each. Package them in 5's or 10's for easy counting. Each ticket is worth a chance on the item being auctioned. Have a cardboard box by each item you sell. Members write their names on as many tickets as they want chances for that particular article. Then they drop the tickets in its box nearby. Of course when the count is taken, the name appearing on the most slips in the box buys that article.

Dutch Auction

As the members bid, they must pay the amount named. For example: If one woman says 10 cents, she must pay a dime even if another woman bids 12 cents—and gets it. In other words, the article brings a total of 22 cents, the 10-cent bid plus the 12-cent bid. Naturally, bids will be kept fairly low, but you'll be surprised at the total you'll get.

Take-a-Turn Bingo

One group plays Bingo at each social period. Each player pays a nickel. The person who Bingo's the first time gets the prize. She, in turn, must buy a prize and take it to the next meeting for the winner. Sometimes there is time for several games of Bingo at a meeting, but only the first winner gets the prize. The president bought the first prize to get the project rolling.

Proverb Sale

Here's a variation of the Sing-Along Auction. Ask members to label their wrapped items with a proverb that might describe the contents. The auctioneer reads the label aloud. Members bid, sight unseen. Their only hint is the proverb or quotation. (Examples: a small dog figurine, "Every dog has his day;" a mirror, "Look before you leap;" a bird-shaped pin cushion, "A bird in the hand is worth two in the bush.") This auction is double-fun. People have lots of fun trying to think of appropriate sayings as they wrap their packages. Then they enjoy it again, guessing at the time of the sale.

Pass-along Auction

Members donate articles for sale—castoffs, baked goods, jewelry, etc. Then instead of bidding aloud, members place their names and bid on a slip of paper and pass it to the right. The auctioneer collects slips of paper from each row of chairs. He checks them, and the highest bidder gets each article.

Chapter Two

SALES FOR THE PUBLIC

Perhaps you can find a gimmick that will just suit your group, and your community.

Big Name Auction

Write to celebrities for donations. There's no guarantee how much loot you'll collect, but it's fun to try. Flatter the hometown-boy-who-made-good with a request, now that he is so famous! He'll probably come through for you. Write movie stars, writers, senators, or anyone you can think of for souvenirs. Just be sure each "name" will be known to the majority of people in your town. Allow plenty for postage and be prepared to get only a few replies.

When the packages arrive, label them with the donor's name in big letters, and sell them still wrapped. People will bid like mad for something — anything — from a celebrity. You'll want to refund if an expensive purchase turns out to be almost worthless when unwrapped. Better designate a judge ahead of time, and explain that his decision is final.

Just Peanuts

Unless a school group already sells peanuts and popcorn at home football and basketball games, why not consider it for your club?

Christmas Trees

If you can arrange to get a carload of Christmas trees whole-sale, it might be a profitable business. However, if local merchants are able to handle the trade, don't try to compete with them. This is especially true in a small town. Cities probably have enough customers that your little business won't hurt the stores much, if any.

Pop-it Profit

A slow, but steady means of income has a minimum of work. A society operated a popcorn machine on a busy street corner twice a week. They bought a second-hand machine. All materials were purchased, and the women worked in shifts. The machine paid for itself in a short time; then all profit went into the treasury. A popcorn machine would also come in handy to make extra money at bazaars, sports, and other public affairs.

Herb Magic

A garden club studied herbs for a series of meetings. As a climax, they held a herb sale. They offered herb plants such as lavender, mint, rosemary, and geranium as well as dried herbs for cooking. During the afternoon they served tea or coffee and tidbits flavored with herbs.

City Memories

You'll enjoy doing research on the history of your town. Search old newspapers, church and school records, and interview old-timers. A member with writing ability can write the history with some help on the facts. The town's citizens not only will buy the history for themselves but for relatives who have moved away.

Have the history printed, illustrating with old pictures if available. Be sure to include old landmarks, names of city officials through the years, the school system, community activities, churches, a street map, etc.

A list of present telephone numbers of the police department, fire department, ministers, and school superintendent might be helpful.

No-work Picnic

No-work Picnic. Sell a ticket that entitles the bearer to transportation, entertainment, and a picnic lunch.

Publicize a picnic that is no work! People buy a ticket that entitles them to transportation (if needed), entertainment, and a picnic lunch. It's prepared by your committee, with donated food. (Well, **somebody** has to work—but not the picnickers who buy the tickets.)

Profit with a Bang

One church group sets up a fireworks stand every year. They begin selling as soon as the city ordinance allows. In their case, it is one week before July 4th. They set up just

Profit with a bang! Church women sell f i r e w o r k s and make p r o f i t for their group.

outside the city limits (another ordinance). Members work in shifts, often as husband and wife teams. It's a once-a-year affair, but they make good money while they're at it.

Christmas Trimmings

This can be a separate sale, or a part of a pre-holiday bazaar. Sell Christmas greenery, tree decorations, gift wrappings, table decorations, place cards, door swags, holiday corsages—everything you can think of. Talented members can make some; others you can buy and sell for slightly more than cost. You might also like to sell Christmas cards.

Between the Acts

Try this sale along with your next play or program. Send out your "talkin'est" member to solicit articles from friends and merchants. Donations might range from an automobile grease job to a box of cake mix. Label packages with a hidden number. Before the play and between acts, sell numbered tickets. After the program, hold a drawing for the numbered prizes.

Birthday Calendars

One church organization makes birthday calendars. Members pay to list names of themselves and relatives on their birth dates. There's no limit as to how many a member can list, just so long as she pays the required ten cents per name. Calendar pages are large with a month to a page. Small ads of local merchants appear at the bottom of each page—more profit. Calendars sell easily and make a handy birthday record.

Birthday calendars bring in money, and make a handy record.

Chapter Three

DONATIONS FROM MEMBERS

Some club women would rather donate money than time and work. It's a good idea to use novel ways to collect the cash. Perhaps some of these will suit your purpose.

Cash Only

Waist Money

Members pay a penny an inch for their waist measurements. Give a shiny new tape measure to the lady who donates the most money!

Just Give

Announce that for one whole season there will be no fund-raising activities. Instead, members will be expected to donate the same amount of money as the usual food, time, and energy for such projects. The women may be glad for a rest!

Blessing Box

Give each member a small box, her blessing box. Whenever she feels especially thankful for something, she drops in a coin. Soon the family, and even guests, get interested and add their offerings. Collect the boxes at the meeting nearest Thanksgiving Day.

Spotty

The club buys a piggy bank. Members take turns keeping "Spotty." Probably one month in each home will be about right. "Spotty" sits in the middle of the table every meal. Any-

Spotty, the pig, teaches table manners.

one who spills during the meal must pay a fine, putting the money into the piggy bank. One woman decided to adopt this method for her own family to save the laundry of tablecloths!

Sunshine and Gloom Bags

Divide members into two teams. Give members of one team a "Sunshine" bag or box in which she is to put a penny every day the sun shines. Other team gets "Gloom" bags to hold pennies for cloudy days. It must be cloudy, or sunshiny— whichever the case may be—for more than an hour of the day to count.

Size 'Em Up

Members pay the same amount as their size bust, dress, shoe, hose, etc. Half sizes count as a whole size. (For example, a 14½ dress would cost 15 cents.)

What's in a Name?

Every member must turn in her **full** name. Then make a list for each member. Announce that everybody must call everybody else by her middle name at a designated meeting. If someone forgets and calls a woman by her regularly-used name, she is fined a penny. This adds fun to the social hour as well as a few cents to the treasury.

Easy-Money Apron

Make miniature aprons, with a pocket on each. On them pin a note with this verse:

> An apron means work,
> That we allow.
> Here's an easy way—
> And this is how:
>
> Measure your waist,
> Give a penny an inch,
> Put inside the pocket.
> (Be sure you don't pinch!)

Then add the name of the organization. Set a certain day as "Apron Day" for members to turn in the donation aprons. Ask them to wear their own aprons that day to add to the fun.

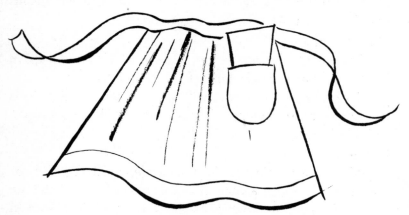

Easy-money apron has a note in its pocket.

The Old Sock

Announce that everybody knows "the old sock" is a favorite place for money. In this case, members pay a penny each for stocking size. (For example: size 10—10 cents.)

Birthday Bank

Many Sunday Schools keep a bank for birthday money. During closing exercises, anyone with a birthday during the week drops as many pennies as years into the bank. The congregation sings an appropriate birthday blessing.

Joseph's Coat

This is a variation that is good for church groups. Make or buy a jacket. Pass it among the members with instructions that each is to hide a coin under a patch. Each is to use a different color for her patch. When the coat finally comes back to the club treasurer, it will look like a coat of many colors. The donations under the patches add to the treasury.

Tote that Bag!

Surprise members as they arrive. Fine them a penny per ounce for their purses. They're not allowed to remove one single thing before they "weigh in." If scales aren't available, fine them a cent for each article in the purse.

Mile of Pennies

Type on envelopes: "Sixteen pennies make one foot. We want to gather a whole mile of pennies! If you put sixteen pennies in this envelope, you will have donated a foot toward the mile we're striving for." Add the name of the organization and to whom the envelope should be given.

Hot Seat

Before each meeting, the hostess decides which of her chairs will be the "hot seat." After all members have arrived and are seated, she announces which is the "hot seat." The woman occupying that chair pays a fine into the club treasury!

Budget Trouble

Another church used posters to point out the purpose of the budget, where each dollar was going, etc. Charts, and sometimes cartoons, dramatized the need for money.

A Fine Time

Warn the members they are to come to the meeting with plenty of pennies. Have extra change on hand. Fine the women as follows:

If wearing red—3 cents

If both shoes match—1 cent

If the mother of more than two children—1 cent

If wearing glasses—2 cents

If she has more than six articles in her purse—4 cents

If she didn't eat an egg for breakfast—2 cents

If she has a name beginning with S—1 cent

If her husband's name is John—3 cents

If she hasn't read a book in a month—3 cents

If she is a club officer—1 cent

If she likes ice cream—1 cent

If she is late—5 cents!

Money for the Sole

A church group mailed small pasteboard "shoe soles" to friends and relatives. The sole was made double so cash could be slipped inside. Instructions written on the pasteboard asked for the same amount as the shoe size of the person donating.

Money for the sole. Make shoe soles of cardboard, two thicknesses. Leave an opening to slip folded note inside.

Musical Hat

The pianist plays as a hat is passed around. Whenever the music stops, the person holding the hat must drop in a dime.

A variation is to have the first time cost a penny, the next two cents, the third a nickel. The fourth—and last—time costs a dime.

See it Now

A Sunday School needed extra funds. Several artistic teachers designed posters soliciting money. The posters were unusual as they featured photographs of various groups. People became interested in finding their pictures, and other familiar faces, in the posters. They usually were glad to drop a cash donation into the plate nearby.

Miscellaneous Donations

Schoolday Tablecloth

PTA members sold autograph space on a tablecloth for a dollar a signature. Persons buying the space wrote their names with ball point pens. Members embroidered the names later at club meetings. When finished, the tablecloth became the property of the school for all their functions. The PTA members took turns laundering it after use.

Schoolday Tablecloth. Sell autograph space on a tablecloth as one PTA did.

Birthday Cake

Each member brings a cake to the meeting nearest her birthday. The pieces are sold at a nickel each and the money goes into the club treasury.

Buy a Snack

Some clubs have a steady little income. It's simple. Members "buy" their refreshments, or give a free-will offering each time. Since the refreshment committee furnishes the food, this method is pure profit.

Secret Pals that Pay

Many groups have secret pals, heart sisters, or whatever they call them. These mystery friends can be money-makers. Women who want to take part list their names, birth date, favorite color, and hobby. These names are sold for ten cents each the first meeting of the year. The usual small gifts and cards are sent by each to her secret pal. At the last meeting, the names are revealed.

Bible Breakfasts

Several church groups sponsor breakfasts, followed by Bible study. The hostess donates the food, and those attending pay the organizations for their breakfast. The breakfasts are held at the same time throughout the city. You may prefer doing them as a series, one a day.

Air Race

Divide your group into teams. Give each the name of a famous airline. Then, at the end of the year, see which "airline" wins the race by turning in the most money. As a climax, have a party at the "airport"—regular meeting place. The losers must do all the work and the "pilots" of the winning team just enjoy themselves.

Cake Magic

Wrap a small object in waxed paper and place in a cake before baking. At refreshment time, sell "guesses" on what is in the cake, at a nickel a guess. Winning guesser gets the object, rather than the woman who gets the piece of cake containing it. Suggestions: ring, thimble, dime, etc.

Unseen Guest

Next time your missionary society has a supper, ask each person to buy a meal for his unseen guest. During the evening she introduces her "guest"—a famous missionary, a native nurse in a foreign hospital, an international church leader. That way, each woman pays the cost of two meals. She eats only one, of course, but donates the money for the other.

Dinner Guests

Members include their husbands in on this plan. The first couple draws the name of another couple which they entertain at dinner. The "guests" pay a total of $2.00 for the meal. This goes into the club treasury. Next, these guests draw the name of another couple, whom they entertain. They pay in the same manner. This goes on until all members have entertained and been entertained. The "host" couple furnishes the food, of course. This project makes a grand way to have an enjoyable evening and to catch up on one's social obligations. In addition, it sometimes means new friends if one couple draws the name of another who are only acquaintances.

Egg Money

If your organization is a rural one, this method is easy. Ask each member to give the eggs, or the price they bring, laid by her hens on club day (or Sunday, if a church organization). One person with an egg crate in the car could make the rounds and soon collect enough eggs for a profitable trip to market.

Take Home Your Supper

Members each take one item of food to the club meeting. The other members buy the food. For example, if Mrs. Brown baked bread that morning, somebody else would love buying a half dozen homemade cinnamon rolls. Husbands like this money-maker because they eat well, even on club day!

Hi, Finance

Give a dime from the treasury to each member. Set a certain time limit for her to "invest" the money at profit. (For example, one woman made a towel from ten cents worth of fabric. Then she took the profit from that and bought ingredients for a cake. The cake sold at a profit that allowed her to buy fabric for an apron. And so it went.) At the final meeting, everybody tells how she increased her original ten cents investment. Give a prize to the woman bringing in the greatest profit.

Bean Patch

This combines entertainment and profit at a club meeting. Give everyone the same number of mixed dry beans, peas, rice kernels, alphabet macaroni, and any other cereals. At the signal, each begins dividing her pile into separate categories. (In other words, all beans in one pile, all rice in another, etc.) Blow the whistle. The player having the largest pile still unsorted pays a fine. Blow the whistle so the group may resume sorting for awhile. Again, at your signal, the player with the largest pile pays the fine. Continue this for several times. Finally, at the last signal, everybody who has any unsorted must pay! Fines should be small—maybe only a few cents.

Penalty Quizzes

Do your women like paper and pencil games? Next time, combine entertainment and money-making. Instead of awarding winners, each player must pay for all her wrong answers!

Lord's Acre

Each farmer is asked to set aside one acre of land. The profits from everything grown on this acre go to the church. The same principle can be used by setting aside a portion of the garden for pulpit flowers, vegetables for the preacher's family, etc.

Traveling Basket

Put several pieces of handcraft or home-baked products in a basket with a small bank. A member takes the basket home. She chooses one of the items and drops money for it into the bank. Before taking the basket to the next meeting, she adds a new article. Thus, the basket is passed from member to member, each buying from the contents and adding to the store. The treasurer empties the bank.

Generous Hostess

One club has been doing this for years. The hostess always prepares some surprise gift before the club meets with her. Chances on this article, sight unseen, are sold at the meeting. You may want to put a limit on the value of the article.

Chapter Four

SERVICES THAT PAY

Grandma Baby Sitters

A club of elderly women set up a baby sitting service. They gave most of their earnings to the club treasury. They watched the babies more for pleasure and to avoid loneliness than for personal profit.

Magazine Subscriptions

Some publishing companies give commissions to organizations for selling subscriptions. Write to the publisher of your favorite magazine to see if he offers such a plan.

Aunt Dinah's Quilting Party

If you have older women in your group who can do quilting, you're lucky. They'll enjoy it, and people will be delighted to pay for hand-stitched quilts. "You can't hardly get them no more!"

Personally, I have some happy memories of playing under the quilt frame while the Missionary Society ladies quilted at our house. And from their chatter, I'm sure it was a social event for them, too.

Sewing Day

An all-day sewing bee is sociable—and profitable. Perhaps husbands can help load, and unload, sewing machines. Have a potluck lunch at noon and rest a bit. Then up and at it again. You can either do new garments, or mending of old ones. At a price, of course.

Float-a-Loan Profit

It is easier to decorate a car or truck for a parade if you make a framework. Use 2x1's or 2x2's, building as shown. Use L-shaped metal braces at all joints to help keep the frame rigid. Measure the truck or car accurately for the exact size you need. Cover frame with heavy wrapping paper or cloth. Add crepe paper decorations, or whatever is desired.

If there's a parade in your town, with a cash prize for the best float, by all means enter it. You might even make money "hiring out" to other groups to design and make their floats.

Old Clothes For Sale

A county project had workshops for rejuvenating old clothing. Ten workshops lasting three days each were held throughout the county. Members ripped, cleaned, and pressed clothes in advance. Then the garments were brought to the workshop and re-styled.

Some women liked the "new" garments so well they bought back their own!

A Stitch in Time

The employed bride, the bachelor, the wealthy woman— all may have mending they'll pay to have done. Do it during club meetings! If mending isn't all finished, perhaps members can take it home to finish.

Beauty Shop

One group of women take turns giving each other home permanents. Some states have a law that a non-professional operator cannot charge for her services. Instead of paying the operator, the customer puts several dollars into the church or club treasury.

Before you give home permanents, check to see if your
state has a law that non-pro-
fessionals cannot charge for
their services.

Swap Shop

Organize a clothes-loaning service for children. Tots outgrow garments so rapidly. The coat that is too short for Nancy may be just right for Betty. Likewise, Susan's coat may be cute as a button on Nancy. And so it goes.

Pay for each garment brought in, and sell it at a slight profit. That will probably work better than "even-steven" swapping.

Wallpapering

One club has a paper hanging committee! They hire out as a team—trimmers, cutters, pasters and hangers. They've had so much practice they make quick work of a room.

Birthday Records

If you have some good storytellers in your group, arrange for them to make records for children. Take orders ahead of time so the narrator can call the child by name. A soloist might sing "Happy Birthday." Some music stores provide a recording service you can rent.

Hat Check Girls

Members of an auxiliary take turns checking hats at a local hotel. You might try the same thing at public events.

Hat check girl. Club members take turns, have fun, and turn proceeds over to the treasury.

Christmas Helpers

If your group has someone who is talented at gift wrapping, pay her a small fee to offer the service. Her fee and supplies—paper, ribbon, etc.—come out of the profits. Somebody may bring in his whole Christmas list of packages for wrapping!

Fair Baby Sitters

Parents of tiny tots will be grateful for this service. Be sure to check with fair officials about space, regulations, etc. Round up some equipment for the playground. If possible, set up a small tent with cots for naps. You'll need an ice chest for cold drinking water and milk. Perhaps a local dairy will provide milk at cost for publicity. A graham cracker company might even furnish their product for snacks.

Buy disposable diapers. You'll also need a toilet.

Members can take turns "sitting" with the youngsters. Provide name tags for all children. Should a child become ill or impossible to handle, page the parents on a public address system. Charge a small fee, by the hour.

Pretty-as-a-Picture Cakes

Women are often willing to pay for a good cake-decorating job. If you have several members with the know-how, pay them a small fee to decorate cakes brought in. If they really

Pretty-as-a-picture cakes. Women are often willing to pay for a good cake decorating job.

enjoy doing it, they may donate their services if the club, or the customer, buys the ingredients.

Rental Services

Art for Art's Sake

How about buying fine paintings or reproductions, and renting them out for a month or so at a time? Perhaps there are amateur painters who would be glad to loan their work, or attics may yield masterpieces. Many people cannot afford fine pieces, but would be glad to pay to enjoy them for awhile.

Patterns for Profit

Many times a woman buys a pattern and uses it only once. She may be glad to donate it, or sell it for a few cents. Set up a pattern service, with a 10- or 15-cent rental fee. Insist that patterns be in good condition. When the pattern is returned, check to make sure all pieces are intact.

S.O.S. Storkline

Have you ever had relatives drop in with a baby, and you've no place to put him? There's always a dresser drawer but that doesn't seem very hospitable! Besides, it holds only a tiny baby. Just think how a rental agency for baby cribs and other equipment would help.

Your organization might sponsor such a service. Members could take turns keeping the cribs, play pens, carriages, etc., clean and in repair. You'll need a storeroom, too, of course.

A doll library will delight little girls — and your club treasurer.

Doll Library

Just think how a little girl—or perhaps even a boy—would like to "check out" a new doll and its wardrobe! Set up a doll library similar to a regular library, with about two weeks as the deadline for the return. Members see to it that shelves are kept stocked, and serve as librarians. You may want to open the library only on Saturday afternoons. Assess a fine for any damage or delay in returning the dolls.

You could use this same idea for a variety of toys, as well as dolls.

Party Pantry

Not many can afford such litttle-used items as elaborate punch bowls, huge coffee urns, tea service, extra linens, folding chairs, and centerpieces. Renting is the ideal solution for a special event such as a wedding or big party. Your club can conduct a rental service. Collect an adequate deposit on each article.

Electrical Appliances

Many young couples can't afford an adequate supply of appliances right off the bat. The bride would probably rather rent a vacuum cleaner than to go over her house with a broom! Floor waxers are good for rental as are a home movie projector, an electric ironer, and an electric roaster for that come-seldom big crowd. Give the service plenty of publicity.

Storytelling

Every youngster loves a story. Try a Saturday morning story hour.

A Saturday morning story hour is fascinating for the children and can bring in a small profit. Don't charge much. You don't want to eliminate children who can't afford a large fee. This charge could include a cookie and milk, about halfway through the morning.

The best storytellers in your club might take turns. Or, if one is particularly adept or trained, pay her a small fee.

Do not get too large a group. You have to be an expert to hold the attention of more than thirty children at a time.

Choosing the Story

It must be suitable to the age level. If there is too wide a range in ages, you may want to break the group into two sections, with a storyteller for each. They can meet in different rooms or at different hours. Check at your library or bookstore on age levels of the various books.

The story should appeal to the imagination, point out a moral, or give a bit of interesting information. A successful story never preaches!

The tale must have action. Children want a story to move, just like they do. Avoid too much description, and choose a story you like yourself.

Be sure the story is slanted to the child's interest. A rural child may enjoy hearing about New York City, but he needs to hear a few familiar words so he won't feel completely lost. Think of the things children in your age group are most interested in, and find stories on those subjects.

Try different types—ghost stories, folks tales, fairy stories, comic stories, adventure stories. Many youngsters are delighted with poetry, especially ballads with a rhythm. It is best not to attempt dialect unless you've had a lot of practice.

Avoid stories that will frighten even one child. If you see signs that a youngster is upset, quietly set his mind at ease.

Then choose future stories with that tot's fears in mind.

And of course you want a happy ending. It gives children a feeling of security to have a story turn out as it should. They can't explain their concern, but it bothers them if a tale turns out too far from the logical ending.

How to Tell the Story

Read it carefully beforehand. Tell it aloud to yourself, in front of a mirror. You do not need to memorize it, but know it well enough so you can look up frequently.

A reader should have a good voice that is easily understood. You need a lot of "expression" in your reading. Even the most exciting story grows dull when read in a monotone.

Keep your voice natural but be sure everyone can hear you. As you begin, ask if you're speaking loud enough. You know yourself how frustrating it is to only half-hear a program. If any one child still has trouble hearing, move him forward.

Sit where you are on a level with your audience. If they're on the floor, sit on a low stool. Look into the faces of each child. Ask a question once in awhile. Forget yourself. Think only about the story and the listeners.

Be sure all the children can see your face. Have you ever tried watching a program from behind a post?

Be enthusiastic but not exaggerated. Don't be afraid to use natural gestures. Children love motion.

Don't ever preach. If the story points a moral, let it stand as is. Don't enlarge on it, except to explain in simple words to the tiniest tots.

Expect interruptions. They are bound to happen with children. Answer questions in as few words as possible, so the thread of the story won't be lost. If there has been some conversation, give a quick summary of the story before you proceed.

Study popular children's TV programs and copy technique. But be sure it is a program the youngsters **really** like—not something they're supposed to like.

Never drag out a story. When you get to the climax, stop!

Discuss the story when you're through. Ask for comments. This makes choosing future stories easier.

Don't be shocked if Johnny says emphatically, "That's a dumb story." Analyze it. Maybe it is, from a little boy's viewpoint. Try to figure out why and avoid that type in the future. However, read what the majority want. Johnny could be putting up a bluff for fear of being called a sissy!

When the series is over, let the children dramatize the story they like best. Invite parents to the dramatization and coffee on the closing day.

Signs of a Successful Story

Did the children listen carefully? Continued restlessness means a poor choice of story or too long a session. Check the room temperature. If it's too hot and stuffy, interest is bound to lag and children become drowsy.

Do the children ask questions, eagerly? Then they must be interested. The sight of a circle of spellbound faces is a great inspiration!

Nursery School

The increase of salaried mothers makes a nursery school a profitable venture, but be prepared for real work! Planning is very important.

Location

If yours is a group church, you might make an arrangement with the church for space on weekdays. Perhaps you have a club house or can rent a vacant building. Be sure there is plenty of playground space outdoors. You'll need adequate toilet facilities, too.

Naps

Be strict about rest periods as tired youngsters quarrel easily. They can nap on mats on the floor.

Finances

If you have no outside help, such as the church or an institution, there is still a good possibility your venture will be a success.

Get as many advance tuitions as possible. If there are needy children, perhaps a charitable organization or a kind friend will pay the tuition.

Ask parents and club members to loan playground equipment to help on that expense. They may also be willing to fix up the classroom. If necessary, sponsor special projects to raise money for equipment.

Time

Several days a week is fine for those children who are sent only to learn crafts and to play with other youngsters. But for those who need a full time "baby sitter," a five-day schedule is a must. Check to see what is most needed in your home town before you decide on days and hours.

Food

If an 8 a.m. to 5 p.m. schedule is maintained, the children's lunch may be somewhat of a problem. If you want to go into it, you might sell the food or include the cost in the fees. Children can bring their lunches from home if that works out better.

Equipment

Ask a specialist to help you decide what is needed. Chances are you'll provide modeling clay, crayons, paste, scissors, etc. A sand table is fun, too.

Teachers and Supervisors

Hire a supervisor for your nursery, and then let her run it! Don't let all the club members "horn in."

It depends on attendance, but one woman and an assistant may be able to handle the work. In checking qualifications, select women who are not only efficient, but who love children. A tiny tot left in the care of strangers while Mommy is working has quite an adjustment.

Additional Information

The chances are your own state department of education can supply you with more material. Write to the Association for Childhood Education, 1200 15th St., N.W., Washington, D. C., for material.

And where does your club or organization come in? You do the planning, equipping, and any necessary cleaning. You might appoint a committee to hire the supervisor. She may want to get her own assistant. You set the fees, and appoint someone—perhaps the treasurer—to collect them. You'll need a budget that allows plenty for expenses. There should be some left over, and of course that goes into your treasury. In addition, you have met a need of your community.

Chapter Five

COMMUNITY AFFAIRS

In addition to bazaars, fairs, and other major projects, there are many smaller affairs that are profitable.

Cake Walk

Ask members to donate cakes. The public comes to buy. The "walk" may be anything from a dance to a grand march.

Fox Drive

One club sponsored a fox drive. They served dinner to the hunters at a nice profit. If hunting is a favorite sport in your community, you might try the same thing.

Movie Time

You can rent films on practically any subject you want. Charge a small admission. Steer clear of the type movies shown at your local theaters, but choose something of interest to your club and community.

Twilight Concert

Perhaps you can remember band concerts in the town square when you were a child. Why not revive the custom? One group sponsored a concert, selling a picnic lunch beforehand.

Old Time Fun

Charades were once as popular as quiz programs are today. They were usually in the form of dramatic skits. A charade evening might be a novelty for your town. Sell tickets. Plant a few people in the audience to ask questions and shout out guesses, to keep things going. The others will soon be chiming in.

You'll probably need about half a dozen actors and a Master of Ceremonies. He should make necessary explanations and hold up cards for any letters that cannot be acted out.

Take Me Out to the Ball Game

If your organization boasts quite a few young women, you may want to form a baseball team. Perhaps other groups in surrounding communities will do the same and you can match games.

If you haven't enough ball - playing members, include daughters and young friends. A slight admission charge should bring in a good profit. You can also set up popcorn and cold drink stands.

Dime Time

Members of one group donated castoffs, wrapped but labeled "man," "woman" or "child." There was a table of each at a Dime Social. A woman stood behind each counter throughout the evening to sell the packages, sight unseen, for a dime each.

Decorations were huge "dimes," made by wrapping cardboard discs with aluminum foil. Several games and contests were held, each with a ten-cent entry fee.

Lunch was sold later in the evening. Cake and coffee cost a dime.

Hayride

Junior high kids love hayrides. And so do other ages! Why not charge a fee for them to ride? Perhaps a rural member has a hayrack and horses. Pay the owner "rent" or a fee to do the driving. The rides may become so popular that you'll find the hayrack frequently in demand.

The hayride could end in a wiener roast. Or you serve lunch in "courses" along the way. The first stop could be at a lady's who serves hot soup, the next at the hamburger stand, the last for dessert. Food can be donated by the members; the youngsters pay as they're served.

Choose the method of serving that best suits the groups—both your club members and the hayriders. If you have it on a chilly autumn evening, prepare for big appetites!

Junior High age kids love hayrides. Your club can make money while the kids have fun.

Sponsor square dances if they're popular in your community.

Swing Your Partner

Sponsor square dances if they're popular in your community. You'll need music, of course. Perhaps there is a small band in your town. Or use records. At any rate, have a good caller, either in the flesh or a record. Charge admission, and sell coffee and doughnuts throughout the evening.

Homecoming

Many schools have alumni banquets or homecoming affairs of some kind. Your club might take over the whole event— planning, entertainment, serving food—for a fee.

Movie-goers

Check with local theaters to see if they might be interested in having you sponsor a worthwhile movie. Your group can sell tickets, give it publicity, etc., for a cut in the admission prices.

Town Fiestas

Do a little research on your community. Is it a Swedish settlement, originally? Then your club should sponsor a Swedish smorgasbord, by all means.

Whatever nationality is represented to any great extent is sure to furnish you with ideas for a traditional celebration.

Spelling Bee

The old-fashioned spelling bee is growing in popularity, after all these years. Make it a public affair, with a small admission. Perhaps your ladies' club would like to challenge a men's club! Give the affair lots of publicity and get the rivalry at high pitch. You might even have a contest to see who buys the most tickets—male or female. The tickets can be two different colors, for easy counting.

A teacher, radio announcer, or minister might pronounce the words. You'll also want a judge with a big dictionary in case any spelling is questioned.

Give a cash prize to the persons standing longest. Perhaps the losing side can give a party to the winners later—or challenge them to another spelling match!

Cotton Pickin'

A ten-acre plot was donated to a Southern church. The stipulation was that members of the church plant cotton and cultivate it, free of charge. All profit goes to the building fund.

Perhaps you can find a generous member to donate a garden plot. Take turns keeping it up, and sell the vegetables.

Debates

Either professional debaters or amateurs can be highly entertaining. Perhaps your high school has a good debate team. Suggest a lively subject and charge admission.

Lectures

If possible, secure the services of a well-known, excellent speaker. Be sure to find out if his fee includes traveling expenses or if that is an additional cost for your club.

Arrange for his hotel reservation unless a club member wants to put him up for the night.

Charge admission, of course, but be sure the speaker is terrific and will appeal to many people.

Garden Exchange

This is particularly good for a garden club. Charge gardeners a small fee to enter the exchange. They bring plants, and trade to their heart's content.

Garden Exchange. Charge gardeners a small fee to enter the exchange. They bring plants, and trade to their heart's content.

Conclude the afternoon with light refreshments that you can easily handle with the facilities available. You don't need to sell the food but have a cup for silver offerings. If you prefer selling the food, then skip an admission charge.

Box Suppers

Once a favorite social event, box suppers can still furnish an entertaining, profitable evening for your club. Women prepare box lunches and decorate the boxes. Men bid on them. High bidders get the box—and its owner as his eating companion. There are many variations to the usual box supper.

Backwards Box Supper

The affair gets a new twist when the **men** bring the boxes, and the ladies bid! It can be hilarious.

Sock Supper

Each woman brings food, such as an apple or a piece of wrapped candy, in one sock of a pair of hose. Instead of bidding on boxes, the men and boys bid on the socks! When all have been sold, the males hunt up the gal with the other sock and the **rest** of the lunch. (The fruit or candy he got in the sock is his dessert!) Then, as a final prize, the man gets to keep **both** socks, making a pair.

Sock Supper is a variation of the old - fashioned box supper. You put the food in a sock!

Basket Lunch

Instead of a box supper, offer baskets of food. They should include accessories such as picnicware, a vacuum bottle, etc. Then hold out for a high price.

Christmas Box Supper

For a change, have the affair during the holiday season. Boxes are "gift-wrapped," and the auctioneer dressed like Santa Claus.

Pet Parade

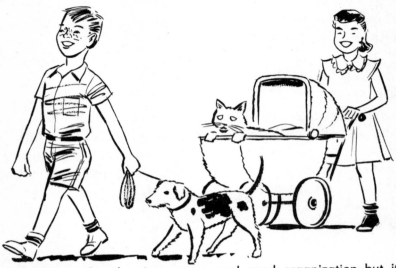

A pet parade takes iron nerves and good organization but it might make money for your club.

This one takes iron nerves and good organization! It can even become an annual event and a community institution. Here are a few rules:

1. Location. Choose adequate space—the park, main street, a vacant lot, the school athletic field.

2. Charge admission and a small entry fee.

3. Have a veterinarian present all during the performance.

4. Rule that all animals must be clean and on a leash or in a cage.

5. It's a good idea to have children under eight years accompanied by parents.

6. Prizes aren't essential, but some kind of ribbons are! Make a great many children happy by including such categories as shaggiest dog, smallest kitten, most unusual pet, and so on and on. You can manage to include all of the contestants in some way.

Sports Tournament

Is your city sports-minded? Perhaps your club, co-operating with others, might sponsor a sports tournament. Suitable sports are baseball, softball, basketball, horse-shoes, bowling, volley-ball, badminton, tennis and dart - throwing. If you are near a lake or large body of water, you might sponsor a tournament for swimming, boating, water-skiing, or ice skating. Perhaps your project can include several sports to interest more people.

The elimination tournament is the simplest. You can even have a consolation play-off between the losing teams. The round-robin method is for major team games but involves organizing teams and leagues. It's almost too big a project to undertake unless several clubs are co-operating. It's usually planned for a complete season of a sport rather than a day's activities.

A full-day sports festival is probably your best bet. It can include a number of games and sports, with something planned for every age.

If you conduct it on a contest basis, you'll need detailed planning. You're apt to get swamped down with attending to time officials, basis for rating, judges, places and equipment, classification rules, and awards. If you keep the affair simple, it will probably be better. Let it be strictly for fun. Relay races and comedy numbers such as a three - legged race between couples or a sack race is popular.

Rummage Sales

Always a favorite money-maker, a rummage sale cleans attics and basements! Plan it well in advance and warn members so they'll be saving up articles to donate. You'll find that spring and fall are probably the best times. As the season changes most women check their clothing and prepare them for storing.

Insist on clean clothing. Accept old dishes, jewelry, trinkets, and shoes. As a rule, hats don't bring in much money.

You may decide the church basement is the best location. However, remember people who patronize rummage sales in large cities may hesitate to enter a church—much as we hate to admit it! If yours is a small town, interested persons probably come to help out more than because of actual need.

An empty business building or a school auditorium may be suitable. Some cities maintain a building, or room, just for the purpose of rummage sales by various organizations. You can usually rent it for the day at a fairly reasonable sum. It has the advantage that the needy watch for sales and go there regularly.

If you have a fairly large membership and plan a rummage sale on a large scale, you may need all these committees:

1. Arrangements. This committee plans the sale, makes the arrangements, sets up counters.

2. Publicity. Use the newspapers, posters, and word of mouth.

3. Pick-up committee. Ask contributors to call the committee if they can't bring donations themselves.

4. Finance. The treasurer can be finance chairman, and cashier the day of the sale. Be sure to have plenty of small change on hand. This committee marks prices, too.

5. Sales. This committee is responsible for plenty of sales-ladies, paper (newspaper will do), string, etc.

6. Clean-up. Be sure the same persons aren't on this two years in succession.

Clothing should be sorted and arranged on racks according to sizes. Set up tables for various classifications. Have extra chairs where customers may sit to try on shoes, or to just rest. You'll need them yourselves before the day is over! Oh yes, have a table of "junk" with a nickel or dime sign.

And why not bundle up any unsold merchandise and give it to the Salvation Army? They'll haul it away for you.

Tours

Charge a small fee for tours of various kinds. If it's an all-day tour, you might sell lunch at noon. Or even an afternoon tour could be followed with light refreshments.

Arty Tour

Sponsor a trip to an art gallery. This is particularly interesting if your group has been studying art. Make the tour available to the public, for a fee.

Home Tour

If members have unusually lovely homes or gardens, they may consent to a tour. Open to the public for a few hours in the afternoon—or evening, if you think the men will be interested. Sell refreshments at one or the gardens or patios. Remember to keep the owners' wishes always in mind. They're doing a big favor to open their homes.

Hobby Tours

These are also popular. You have no worry about moving valuable collections to a central location. Hobbies remain in their usual surroundings and visitors come to look.

A collector of antique glass would rather show it in a table setting in her own dining room than to haul it clear across town.

Sometimes people have special space built for a collection. That adds a lot to the appearance of the objects. You couldn't get the same effect with makeshift shelves in some hall. And if gardening is the hobby, it's best to see the whole garden than a few flowers picked from it.

A tour may allow you to show more hobbies than at a regular hobby show.

E-B Day

In one city the teachers (Education) visit various businesses (B). Then the next year, the procedure is reversed. The businessmen visit the city schools. You could promote the same sort of project. Finish the tour with a dinner. Sell tickets beforehand that include the tour and the meal.

Know Your Town

Sell tickets to a tour. Provide a guide who is up on the history and interesting facts about the city. If your city has historical spots, you're lucky. Try to find some little-known facts about them.

Floral Contest

One city-wide observance was in the form of a contest. Churches competed with each other on beautiful decorations. That afternoon one of the church groups sponsored a tour before all the flowers and decorations were taken down.

Chapter Six

PROFITABLE TEAS

A tea is a favorite of many women. Ask members to donate food and the silver offering will be all profit.

A program is not necessary and sometimes even a little awkwards if guests are standing about, sipping tea. Instrumental music in the background adds atmosphere.

If the afternoon does call for a program, wait until all the guests are served so there will be less confusion. Avoid long speeches and present music, both instrumental and vocal.

General Suggestions

1. A table with attractive silver, china, centerpiece, and linen. Spread your tea table with the prettiest cloth you can borrow! Lace, appliqued organdy, fine embroidered linen, or rayon satin damask in white, ecru, or pastel shades are all lovely.

Fig. 1

2. A hostess or receiving line to welcome guests. A receiving line is composed of the hostess or committee chairman, club officers, and special guests.

3. Someone to pour. This honor may be given to club officers, a relative or friend of the honored guest, or anyone you wish to give special recognition.

4. Someone responsible for keeping coffee and teapots filled. Place the pot on a doily-covered tray.

5. Someone to keep supply of china on table. Place the cups with handles toward the person pouring, at her right. Dessert plates are at her left. She fills the cup, puts it on the plate, then hands it to the guest with the handle to the guest's right. Guest then moves on down the table, filling her plate. See Fig. 1 for a tea table arrangement.

6. Someone to keep plenty of **all** supplies on the table. If dishes and silver are limited, keep a dishwasher going in the kitchen.

7. A small table nearby where used dishes may be placed. They should never be placed on the tea table.

8. Finger foods only, unless there are seating arrangements. It's not easy to balance a cup, a plate, and manage to eat with a fork—all while standing.

9. An uncluttered tea table. It's better to replenish supplies frequently than it is to stack cups and plates.

10. Color in the food as well as the decorations.

11. A choice of beverages. Most "teas" offer coffee, too. If weather is warm, you might serve iced tea. A punch bowl makes a lovely centerpiece for a summer event.

Menu for Tea

Tea   Coffee
Assorted Party Sandwiches
Tea Cakes or Dainty Wafers
Salted Nuts   Mints

The above menu is merely a suggestion. You may not want to include all the food given. Do keep everything pretty and dainty, regardless of what you serve. A tea is no place for huge ham sandwiches and giant oatmeal cookies!

Decorations

Use flowers throughout the rooms. A tea is the best excuse for buying flowers your group will ever have. However, members may have flower gardens to help you out.

The final perfect touch is the centerpiece. Of course it should blend in with your color scheme, the china, and linen. The centerpiece can be an arrangement of flowers, flanked with candles or delicate figurines. If an autumn affair, you might even do a combination of 'mums and fruit that is quite effective.

Remember, a decoration that is small and has simple lines is more effective than one that seems to crowd the table. The tea table centerpiece can have more height than one for a dinner table where guests are seated. Whatever you choose, keep it simple.

If you use candles, it's usually best to use at least four. Place them in a balanced arrangement on either side of the center-piece, at each end, or group them together. Candles must be lighted—always.

The following centerpieces may suggest ideas to fit in with your occasion, color scheme, and the flowers that are available:

1. May basket or wide-brimmed, shallow hat filled with flowers.

2. Red or pink carnations in white milk-glass container.

3. Feather carnations and lilies-of-the-valley in dainty arrangement with a fan in the background (if the tea table is against a wall).

4. Yellow and bronze tulips, cut with some leaves for a natural effect, yellow roses in a brown container.

5. Seasonal flowering branches such as apple blossoms.

6. Flowers to match the floral design on the china.

7. Pussywillow branches and narcissus or daffodils. Pretty in a grey or yellow container.

8. Yellow tulips, daffodils, and snapdragons on a pale green cloth.

9. Nasturtiums and leaves in a blue bowl.

10. Mixed petunias in a grey container.

11. Jonquils in a low glass bowl. Center it in a large round glass plate of violets arranged to make a border for the jonquils.

12. Ivy circled around a lovely figurine.

Themes

A tea seldom needs any further "dressing up." However, you might like to work out a theme for added interest and publicity purposes. Take your choice!

Book Review Tea

The reviewer may speak before tea is served. Another friendly, informal way is to sit around in a circle, sipping tea and listening to the review. Be sure the book is good, and the reviewer better! You can either charge an admission or have a container for free-will offering.

Family Treasures

Many women have family heirlooms—lovely dishes, crystal, silver—that they don't get to display often. They'll probably be glad to help with this tea.

Use card tables, with a hostess at each one. She either furnishes the table appointments or borrows them. It is her responsibility to arrange a pretty table setting for four. She is also responsible for washing the dishes and returning them. She may invite whomever she wishes to sit at her table with her (three other women). Give them a chance to browse around and see the heirlooms on the other tables before serving time.

You might provide waitresses or ask the hostess to serve her own table. Serve the lightest of refreshments and tea—hot or iced, depending on the weather.

Each guest drops an offering into a dish. Or you can ask for a specific amount when you invite the guests.

Shakespearean Tea

Shakespeare Week was April 1 to 8 in 1956. Check to see when it is the current year, and plan a Shakespeareans tea. One cultural group had a lovely affair.

The event was held in the afternoon. That same evening "Much Ado About Nothing" was given by college players. So the tea helped publicize the play.

The leading lady, Beatrice, did the pouring. She was dressed in the same costume she wore that night. The beverage was a cooling punch made with American ginger ale and lime sherbet. If in the winter, you could have a Wassail bowl. All the cookies and tidbits were English imports.

Flowers about the room were the type to be found in an English garden. A violinist provided music appropriate to the times. She could have been in costume, too, along with the hostesses, and possibly even the guests. A Shakespearean tea can be as simple or as elaborate as you wish.

The speaker was a college English instructor. He told of his visits to Stratford on the Avon in England; Stratford, Canada, and the newer Stratford, Connecticut. (Shakespeare's plays are given at all three locations.) The speaker showed pictures of the theaters, casts, etc.

Garden Tea

An outdoor tea is lovely in the summer. Iced tea or punch with tiny sandwiches or cookies can be served on a terrace or patio. Have guests sit at card tables scattered around the lawn.

Rainbow Tea

For entertainment—and money—each guest lists her favorite color. Announce that each color costs money! After the woman has "paid for her color," by dropping coin in the pot by the centerpiece rainbow, read the meaning of her choice.

1. White. You are kind, pure, and sweet.

2. Blue. You are imaginative, but are apt to be moody.

3. Pink. You are happy but sometimes shy. You hate arguments.

4. Green. You are quick of temper but witty.

5. Yellow. You are friendly and sociable but inclined to yakety-yak.

6. Purple. You like luxury and are ambitious.

7. Brown. You are a sensible, hard worker.

8. Orange. You are warm-hearted but don't let anyone push you around.

9. Red. You are full of pep but you are apt to be impulsive.

Carry out the rainbow theme in all your decorations. Use pastel-colored flowers, napkins, mints. Arch a rainbow of crepe paper, on a cardboard base, over the tea table. Have tiny pots of gold at each end.

If you want further entertainment, give each guest a typed Rainbow Quiz. Each fills it in as best she can. At the end of the afternoon, give a package of rainbow-hued washcloths or mints as prize.

1. —————————wood Forests, California   (Red)
2. ————————— Hills, South Dakota   (Black)
3. ————————— Mountains, New Hampshire   (White)
4. —————————stone Park, Wyoming   (Yellow)
5. ————————— Gate Bridge, California   (Golden)
6. ————————— Mountains, Vermont   (Green)
7. ————————— Free State, South Africa   (Orange)
8. ————————— Ridge Mountains, Virginia   (Blue)
9. ————————— Coast, Africa   (Ivory)
10. —————————stone River, Montana   (Yellow)
11. ————————— Valley, Nevada   (Ruby)
12. ————————— Sea, Europe and Asia   (Black)
13. ————————— Grass State, Kentucky   (Green)
14. ————————— Sea, Korea and China   (Yellow)
15. ————————— River Valley, North Dakota   (Red)

Musical Tea

Provide a lovely musical background throughout the afternoon. In addition, you might want to carry out the musical theme in your decorating. The centerpiece can be a treble clef (glued onto pasteboard) with small blossoms of flowers as "notes." Or use an arrangement of miniature musical instruments. A violin-shaped wall vase would be an appropriate centerpiece, too. Lay it on the table, with flowers spilling out, or support it so it will stand upright.

Galloping Tea Party

The club members surprise one of their group by all dropping in at once for tea or coffee. The hostess provides entertainment and refreshments.

One group drew numbers so each "hostess" would know which month she might expect her unexpected guests—but not the exact day. Each guest drops in a dime during the party.

A variation is for a hostess to invite four other women to tea or morning coffee. She furnishes the food and each guest pays a quarter that goes into the club treasury. Then each woman who attended invites three of her friends to her house. Her guests do likewise. This continues until every club member has "galloped" to at least one tea party.

"Come As You Are!"

This is a successful favorite. Someone drops in at an early hour, inviting guests to come exactly as they are to a morning coffee. If the invited guest changes her clothes, puts on lipstick, takes the pins out of her hair, or makes any change—she is fined! Even if she stays just as she is, she is expected to drop a coin into the fund. This can be loads of fun.

Party for a Teapot

One clever hostess invited guests to a "birthday party" for her antique teapot. She claimed the teapot was fifty years old that day! Each guest was to bring her favorite antique dish. If she had none, then she was asked to bring any dish or glassware that was a conversation piece. Each was asked to tell the story of her dish, and was served from the birthday teapot. Your club might use the idea, with the usual silver offering.

This would be particularly good if guests brought only antique teacups. Then they drink the tea from their own cups.

Chapter Seven

MONEY-MAKING PARTIES

There are several ways you can make a profit from parties and socials. First, you can charge an admission. Or you can collect forfeits from losers in the games played. You can always sell refreshments. Next time your club plans a social, try to think of novel ways to get at least a few cents from everyone.

You've been to parties yourself where everyone had a marvelous time. Then you have attended others where nothing seemed to turn out quite right. In between is the party that is just so-so. It isn't a complete failure and yet everybody felt a little indifferent. Any group can soon ruin its party-giving reputation with very many of the last two kinds. There are a number of general rules to help make a party successful.

1. Make definite plans. Don't ever say, "Why don't we have a party and make some money sometime?" Decide what kind, when, and all about it.

2. Delegate authority. Have someone who is in **charge.** And be sure that person is appointed ahead of time. Don't say, "Oh, well, we'll think of some games when we get there."

3. Slant to the guest-list. Even a few years difference in ages can make a decided difference in interests. If you're planning

a party for your own age group, do the things you most enjoy. If it's an older, or younger group, be sure and consult with someone of that age. If husbands are included, you'll need a little different approach than if it's a women-only affair.

4. Balance the evening. If you have several active games, also have several sit-down kind.

5. Include mixers where everybody participates, even if only in some small way.

6. Give several people a chance to help with the planning or to appear on the program. Anyone is more interested in a project she has toiled over.

7. Plan parties around a theme. It helps you think of ideas for decoration and publicity. What's more, it ties together a number of miscellaneous, unrelated events.

For example, if you're having an Easter rabbit party for youngsters, vary the old "Tail on the Donkey" game. Instead let the children pin a fluff of cottontail on a rabbit! See how easy it is to change an old game to fit a certain theme?

8. When the party is over, end it! Stop every game while people are still enjoying it. Never give it a chance to lag. End the party the same way—with everyone wishing it weren't over.

Harmony Party

The whole idea is based on tables decorated to illustrate song titles. Plan from ten to fifteen tables, depending on the room and expected attendance.

Appoint a hostess responsible for each table. She decides on a song title, decorates her table to represent the song, and invites three guests.

You'll need a general chairman. She gets the names of the songs to be represented from each hostess. In case a song is already chosen, she asks the hostess to select another. Try to keep everything secret. Even the hostesses won't know what the others are planning until the night of the party.

Table chairmen should arrive about thirty minutes early to set up their tables. Card tables should be large enough. The ideas for decorations are limitless. For example, a doll at one corner could have a flashlight, center, pointing at her. "Brighten the corner where you are!" Or a toy stove could have a picture of a house on top of it. "Home on the Range." You'll enjoy thinking of decorations.

Each table is numbered. When guests arrive, they are given paper and pencil. They circulate among the decorated tables, writing down their guesses of the songs represented.

It may take from thirty to forty-five minutes for everyone to get around to all the tables. As long as people are enjoying the guessing, let them continue. When things begin to slow down a little, ask them to be seated at their hostesses' tables.

Call on the hostesses in numerical order. She stands and tells the name of her song. Contestants check their lists. Give a prize, such as a mouth harp, to the person with the most correct titles.

Following the contest, each table presents its song in some way. This can be pre-arranged by the hostess. Two might sing the song as a duet. Or perhaps the four could "act out" the song. There are many ways of doing it.

Refreshments are served following the program. A kitchen committee prepares the food but each hostess serves her own table.

The guests can pay their hostess a set price, or drop coins into a container on the table.

Two-Generation Parties

Sometimes it's a problem of "what shall we do with the children." A PTA sponsors two-generation parties. Parents and children are entertained at the same time, but in separate rooms. This idea is especially good in the country, where children must be delivered and called for by parents.

Swing Your Partner

Charge admission or sell lunch at a square dance. A schoolhouse with movable seats is grand. One club holds square dances in the courthouse corridor! Perhaps a church basement, barn, the school gym, or a lodge hall will be your best location.

The evening's entertainment should be well-planned with plenty of activity. Yet the program should not be so rigid it can't be changed. If everyone is having a hilarious time, they'll resent your suggestions to swing into something else.

Spot the talent ahead of time. Get the co-operation of teenagers by having them demonstrate a new game. Chances are there's a man who "calls a mean square dance" or who "can make a fiddle talk" if you can find him.

Guests should wear shirts, jeans, and print dresses. Flat shoes are usually more comfortable for the women than high heels.

Get the party off to a good start with a mixer. Try the United Nations Handshake. Players form two circles, one inside the other, facing. When the music stops, everyone shakes hands with the person facing him.

You call out **how** they should shake hands.

By the time people have gone through the following silly handshakes, there isn't much stiffness and formality left!

American—a hearty, "Hi, kid!" with a pump-handle shake.

English—a two-finger greeting and "Cheerio."

French—partners first touch left cheeks, then right cheeks.

Chinese—the solemn shaking of one's own hand.

After this, lead into singing games such as Jolly is the Miller, Pawpaw Patch. If the group prefers square dancing, spend the remainder of the evening dancing. Be sure to have a good caller.

Everybody's Birthday Party

This takes twelve tables. If floor space is limited, set only six tables ("two months" at each).

At this party, families or dates can't sit together! Each guest must sit at his "birthday" table. Reservations, with birth month, should be made ahead of time so the committee will know how many to seat at each table. Have an extra plate or two at each.

Have a simple centerpiece appropriate for the month represented. It's nice to have place cards, too.

Food can be donated by club members. Each guest pays a set price for his plate. Or you might charge everyone a penny for each year of his life!

Commercial Parties

Many companies sponsor parties for demonstrating their wares. Some make most attractive offers to women's clubs.

Fortunes

Here is a good money-making game for any time but especially for a Halloween party. Each pays a dime for his "fortune." But there's more than money involved! Before the party, wind cords over furniture, doorways, etc. At the end of each string is a fortune. Each guest follows a cord to his fortune.

It helps if each string is a different color. Players must never let go of their strings or they may find someone else claiming the same one! After everyone has reached a fortune, each reads his aloud.

Wedding Anniversaries

This is good for an all-church supper or guest night for club husbands. Appoint a hostess for each table. She is in charge of decorations, entertainment, and planning.

Each couple makes reservation in advance, giving their wedding date. Divide the crowd as best you can. You may include all of those married in the last five years at one table, the last ten at another, and so on. Work out whatever divides the group the most evenly.

Before the serving, guests mill around voting on their favorite table decorations. You might offer a prize for the best table.

Of course the hostess stimulates conversation at her table. She introduces any who don't know each other.

The program can feature an excellent speaker. During the program, award prizes for table decorations. Give special recognition to the youngest and oldest married couples, couple with most children, couple who have been members of the church or club the longest.

If a church group, ask couples to join hands while the minister repeats the wedding vows.

Round Robin Parties

These are for club members. However, you can include husbands and give the parties in the evening. Guests pay the hostess an admission fee. She supplies the refreshments as her donation. Entertainment can be games, cars, or TV viewing. Next time, another member is hostess, and so on.

Card Parties

If yours is a card-playing community, this is a good money-maker. One club even sponsored card marathons!

First, appoint a general chairman. She in turn appoints others to be responsible for tables, chairs, cards, ash trays, tallies, and pencils. You'll also need a committee for prizes. Be sure to give them a price range. You may be able to talk merchants into donating prizes. If you wish, have door prizes as well as prizes for winners. Booby prizes add to the fun.

Sell tickets in advance to be sure you have complete tables.

Tickets can be numbered for the door prizes. Give the whole affair lots of publicity.

You might want to have a table or two of Scrabble, dominoes, and other games for non-card players.

Lucky Seven Social

Have it on the 7th of any month, at 7 p.m. Charge 7c admission. Games can all tie in with the number, too. Give a "Lucky Seven" (seven pieces of candy in a sack) to lucky people. They are: every child who is 7 years old, every couple married 7 years, and every couple who has 7 children.

One game could be, "Seven things I like to do" but each must be spelled with seven letters. "Seven of my pet peeves," each with seven letters. Here again the prize can be seven of something or other.

Button, Button Party

Make your invitations with buttons. Glue a 2-eyed button on a white correspondence card. When the glue has dried, make a "button face." Add a bit of brown embroidery thread for hair, a scrap of fabric for a hat, another for a scarf. A dot of red with a crayon makes the mouth. You'll have fun using bits of lace, paper, ribbon . . . all sorts of things. It's surprising how many different button people you can turn out. These make clever place cards, too.

Placecard for a "Button, Button Party" that can be a money-maker.

As the guests arrive, they pay a nickel to guess how many buttons are in a glass jar. At the end of the evening, award the nearest guesser a card of shiny new buttons.

Play all the games you can think of with buttons involved—"Button, button, who's got the button," dropping buttons into a milk bottle from a specified height, pushing buttons along a given line with a pencil, etc. For a sit-down game, have them write down answers as you read these questions:

1. What is a button animal? (goat)
2. What garment should you button up? (button up your overcoat)
3. What order means "keep still"? (button your lip)
4. What is a person doing who interferes? (buttin' in)
5. What is a party game? (button, button, who's got the button?)
6. What shoes are old-fashioned? (button shoes)
7. What tool would be unknown to our children? (button hook)
8. What song was popular a few years ago? (Buttons and Bows)

It would be most amusing for the men to have a race to see which one could sew on a button the fastest!

Refreshments are button cookies and coffee. Put white frosting on any round cookies, adding "eyes" for the buttons with a bit of chocolate. Make extra cookies for take-home buying.

Lemon Squeeze

A lawn social is more interesting if you give it a theme. Try a "Lemon Squeeze!" Use lemons in publicity and decoration. Make plenty of good, iced lemonade and cookies to sell.

Set up a "lemon tree." Each lemon is made of cotton and wrapped with yellow crepe paper. But inside is a fortune, or a small prize. Sell these "lemons" at a nickel each.

Backwards Party

This one is really an oldie! But it usually goes over in a big way. It's certainly the height of informality, as it's all nonsense.

Invitations should be written backwards. Guests can struggle over them, trying to figure them out. If they're written in longhand, all that's needed is to hold them before a mirror.

Write invitations backward, for a Backwards Party. The secret to reading them is: hold them before a mirror!

You can even ask guests to wear some part of their wearing apparel backwards to add to the fun.

When they arrive, a notice on the front door directs them to go to the back. There the hostess shakes the left hand and says, "Good-bye. Here's your hat." The hat she hands each is a party hat, labeled with the guest's name written backwards. These are worn all evening.

Of course at a backwards party refreshments are served first, instead of last. Guests also pay **before** they eat. A sign looks like 90. But before anyone can walk out at the expensive food (90c for ice cream and cake), the hostess turns the sign around. It was backwards, and each pays 9c only.

Try to think of all the games you can where something is done backwards. Relays must be run backwards. Losers, not winners, get the prizes!

As the guests leave, they pay their admission . . . 13c.

Seasonal Parties

Such occasions as Halloween, Christmas, etc., are naturals for parties. See if you can't think of some gimmick to make money-makers out of holiday parties. The decorating and entertainment are easy. What can you do with the profit?

Around the World in Two Hours

This is a popular money-maker. If your group has enough members, why not try it? Sell tickets to the public. Arrange to have about four or five different homes be a different "country." If the hostess is of foreign descent (no matter how remote) all the better. Perhaps she has family heirlooms to add to the effect.

Choose the countries that will be the easiest for your group to plan. The following are merely suggestions:

Sell tickets at the "station"—the church basement, schoolhouse, or wherever you choose. Tickets are numbered and labeled with countries to be visited. Be sure this list of countries appears in a different order so all visitors will not be at the same country at the same time. In other words, some of the tickets may lead off with France, others with Sweden, and so on. Numbers make it easy to tell how many you have sold and also serve as an extra bonus to the travelers!

First Stop Is France

Here guests sit at card tables set up to represent the outdoor sidewalk cafes. The food is French Onion Soup, served with cheese croutons. The hostess calls out the prize-winning number. If that group of travelers does not bear the number on any of their tickets, the hostess waits for the next arrivals and tries again. This same procedure is done at each country. The prize should be some inexpensive object that is suggestive of the country.

Next Stop Is Sweden with a Smorgasbord style table of cheese, a platter of sardines and crackers. The Swedish flag is blue and yellow—a pretty color scheme for your decorations. The hostess here should wear a full peasant skirt, a black-laced bodice, a small white cap, and an apron.

Now for Italy and big steaming bowls of spaghetti! Serve with hard-crusted rolls and relishes. And on to Hawaii with a pineapple sherbet and wafers. And don't forget to make plenty of leis for the travelers! Still time left on your two-hour schedule? Plan some games or dancing. Announce the prize-winners of the trip.

Hostesses at each "country" should dress the part. Decorations and food should also be appropriate. You'll have fun thinking of changes to suit your purpose. Maybe you'd prefer a stop at China, for example, with some wonderful chop suey or chow mein for the main course instead of Italian spaghetti.

This makes a festive evening without too much work for anyone. Each hostess may appoint several to help her with the food and decorations. An even more elaborate evening could include an appropriate short program at each stop. In that case, your trip might be a three-hour one.

Give this party plenty of publicity. It's a natural for gay posters and that sort of thing.

Try it in your group—and happy traveling!

Chapter Eight

CARNIVALS AND EXHIBITS

Such festivities as carnivals, exhibits, fairs and festivals are usually popular with the public. There's always an air of festivity in the air and the money begins to flow freely! Such projects take more planning than minor activities but usually result in more profit.

Summer Carnival

Instead of the usual affair inside the school gym, church basement, or club rooms, plan a summer carnival outdoors. Use the school athletic field or an empty lot.

Arrange for balloon vendors to wander around, selling balloons. Have a record player going for atmosphere. Keep it tuned down to background music, rather than a blare of noise.

If at night, string up lights. Set up a number of booths. Remember, people will spend lots of dimes for many different things where they won't pay a big price for one big item.

Make booth awnings of stripes of colored paper. Sell white elephants at one, play Bingo at another. Set up a "game of chance" where players toss a ball at a target, or something similar. Prizes can be donated by merchants. And of course you'll have one booth of food. A popcorn machine on the grounds brings in profit, too.

Summer carnival. Arrange for a balloon vendor to wander around selling balloons.

Give the whole thing a real carnival air. It's a natural for publicity, especially posters.

Freak Show

Have fun with a freak show and take in some money besides. You'll need a room or tent, a small platform, and a witty master of ceremonies. And of course the freaks! Label a big striped tomcat as a wildcat, sew an extra head on a toy dog for a two-headed dog. Members can dress as the fat lady, living skeleton, etc. Charge an admission and sell food on the grounds.

Country Store

Your group might like to sponsor a "country store." You'll be surprised how many merchants are willing to donate merchandise for an affair of this type. Ask your husbands to set up counters and makeshift shelves. Of course they'll make sure they aren't too makeshift to hold their loads. Try to arrange products to resemble the old-time grocery store. Remember, it included a little bit of everything.

In addition to local businessmen, manufacturers sometimes are willing to donate to causes such as yours. After all, it's good publicity for them. Have someone in the club who can type a neat letter write to them. Be brief and courteous, explaining the project and what the profits will be used for. Make it plain that any samples, no matter how small or how few, will be very much appreciated! Also re-assure them you'll display placards giving credit.

The women can take turns at being "clerks." You might even get aprons for them from a flour company, in typical grocery clerk fashion. Try to price everything at a fair price. The public may be willing to pay a few cents more for a worthy cause, but probably only a few pennies.

Just for effect, you might want to add some real old-time touches, such as a cracker barrel, a pot-bellied stove, scales, etc. Perhaps somebody's attic or basement has some real antiques that might have appeared on Main Street!

A big cracker barrel makes a good "grab bag." In it put paper sacks of samples—cereals, cosmetics, or whatever you've been able to get hold of. Members might start sending in coupons months ahead of time.

As the day wears on, you may want to tag some slow-moving merchandise at cut rate prices.

Don't turn down anything people want to donate. One store like this had an old-fashioned victrola and a box of live baby kittens who needed a home!

You might want to sell food, too. A big old iron kettle is grand to serve from. Use tin pie pans for plates. Serve coffee in mugs.

Ask old timers for ideas of the appearance and products of a typical country store. You'll have lots of fun working it up and should make a nice profit.

State Fair

Why not decorate carnival stands to represent the states? Here are a few suggestions; you take it from there!

Florida—land of flowers. Potted plants; ivy; African violets, etc. Use a trellis and lots of flowers, real or artificial, for decorations. Maybe you could borrow potted palms.

Nevada—ranch country. Sell potted cactus, toy guitars, cowboy hats. Maybe members could make small boys' cowboy outfits to sell. Decorate the booth to look like a desert. Attendant dresses as a cowboy.

California—fruits and vegetables. Use a gay awning overhead; the attendant is in Mexican costume. Make the booth resemble an outdoor market.

Alabama—the cotton state. Here you'll sell cotton aprons and other articles. Use lots of cotton for decorating. The booth can be all white. The attendant could be in blackface.

South Carolina—southern plantation. This is the dining end of the hall. Build artificial "pillars" in the background to look like the porch or front of a southern mansion. Card tables are set about on the plantation "lawn."

Use your imagination and you'll think of lots of novel ideas.

Ranch Fair

Transform the hall into ranch country. Attach paper "mountains" to the walls, with Scotch tape. Add fence posts, railings, and pots of cacti. Booths are around the walls. The center space is the "corral." This gives space for people to mill around.

Decorate the booths with wagon wheels, steer heads, lariats, cowboy hats, etc. Attendants should be in Western attire.

Sell a barbecued dinner in a fenced-off spot. Use the ranch idea on everything you can.

Disneyland Fair

Have famous Disney characters to sell tickets, serve as guides, etc. You might include a Davy Crockett, Mickey Mouse, and others. Adventureland can be several contests, Wonderland an unusual display, Tomorrowland can be fortune telling booth, Fantasyland can be the cafeteria with waitresses dressed as fairies or elves.

Quilt Show

Exhibit some of the lovely work done by women of your club or church. Award prizes, as you open the show, with speeches of congratulations to the prize winners. Keep quilts on exhibit all day and evening.

You'll need these committees:

Collection

Finding the town's best quilts is no small job. Ask for them through church bulletins, newspapers, and by word of mouth. Arrange to pick up any quilts that the owners can't deliver.

Be sure each quilt has a tag, with a duplicate for the owner. It should list the owner's name, the design of the quilt, the name of the maker (if different than the owner), the date made. Each quilt should have a number.

Classification

The committee records owner's name and address, along with the quilt number. The committee members also decide into which classification quilts should go (unless the owner has already specified a choice). This classification number is recorded, too. Attach a card to the quilt.

Awards Committee

This committee gets judges (or even serves as judges if not familiar with the quilts). The members have ribbons made. Awards can be: oldest quilt, most unusual, best workmanship, made by youngest person, etc. Classifications can be: old quilts, new quilts, quilts made by children, quilts made by person over 70 years old at the time of making it. Each classification can be further broken down to appliqued, tied, quilted, and so on, if you have many entries.

Display

This committee is responsible for arranging the quilts. Cards listing interesting facts about the quilt are pinned on, after the awards have been made. Judges are not to know whose quilts they judge, so all information except numbers should be left off until they are through. Be sure to separate new quilts from the old.

The display committee also sees to the safety of the quilts. It is advisable to hang quilts high enough that they cannot be handled. They show to best advantage when hung full length from wires stretched along the walls. Or, if possible, strung across the room about twelve feet apart. No. 12 galvanized wire is best, stretched tightly as possible. If wire is impractical, quilts can be hung along the walls. Never tack through the quilts.

Fasten the quilts securely. The best device is one with a clip on one end to grip the quilt, and a hook on the other end to go over the wire. Stout safety pins also can be used. It takes five huge safety pins for each quilt.

Publicity

Play up any unusual facts about any of the quilts. Perhaps you'll get a good story from a family joke about one quilt, if another has the same design as one owned by a famous person, interesting the history of another.

Refreshments

If possible, serve a silver-collection tea. Or you might simply charge for the refreshments. Another method is to include the food in the sale of the tickets.

Exhibits

People like to look at exhibits, just milling around, taking their time. There is sure to be something of interest in your community well worth putting on display.

Arts and Crafts

Display the work of anyone in the community, regardless of whether it is by club members or not. Invite professional artists and hand-crafters to participate, if they wish. They may be glad to do so, for the publicity. Have judges for both the professionals and amateurs. They shouldn't be judged together. Charge a nominal entry fee.

Fun After 60 Hobby Show

One city gave special recognition to its older citizens. They had their very own hobby show! Displays ranged from homemade soap to professional oil paintings, from stamp collections to antique furniture. White-haired ladies smiled with pride as they explained an intricate embroidery stitch, a scrapbook, or how to make ceramics.

A program featured elderly persons, too, and they did a grand job. This took care of those whose hobbies were "music" or "recitin'."

Refreshments were furnished by local organizations.

Materials and labor were mostly donated, with a few expenses coming out of the profits. There was an extremely small entry fee. All those who had exhibits were then given a free ticket of admission. Others paid to get in, but refreshments were free.

Best of all, every hobbyist received a ribbon of some kind, even if only for participating!

Mixed-up Memories

Most women have a box full of dried corsages pretty sea shells, snapshots, and other mementoes. Why not ask each member to bring her most unusual souvenir to a special display? She could also give the committee a brief explanation (written or typed) of her keepsake.

Number each entry. Before the show begins, the audience browses around. They write down their names and their guesses of the origin and purpose of each souvenir—by number. These are dropped in a box. They're removed by the judges who announce the winners at the close of the show. Naturally those with the most guesses right, win.

The money-making angle comes from a small admission, selling refreshments, or a free will offering. Take your choice.

Stoles—the Show

Each guest wore a stole or shawl of some kind and paid an entry fee. She filled out a registration blank ahead of time. This gave a brief history of the stole, its age, and any other interesting facts. These registration blanks were turned in when the guests arrived.

Contestants wore the stoles all evening, to be admired and commented on. They were real conversation-makers. At the end of the evening, awards were given. Recognized were the oldest, the most interesting, the most beautiful, the newest, etc.

There were no cash prizes—just ribbons. Guests who didn't enter the contest enjoyed the evening, too. They gave a small donation when served lunch later in the evening.

Festivals

If yours is an area well-known for a particular product, use that as the theme for a festival.

Big Apple Festival

If there are many apple orchards, have a festival while the crop is at its peak. Rent space for local growers to display their baskets of apples. Your club women could make applesauce and apple butter and sell it to customers to take home. Use gay booth decorations in keeping with the theme. Attendants can wear bright aprons with big apples appliqued on the pocket. You might even want a stall for selling apple pie, dumplings, and coffee for on-the-spot eating. Recorded music will add to the atmosphere.

Variations are a blueberry festival, strawberry festival, wheat festival, etc. Use the idea for decorations, foods, publicity.

Watermelon Festival

When watermelons are at their best—and cheapest—give a watermelon feed. Have contests and races. Some might be: the usual sack race, stringing watermelon seeds, rolling a watermelon along a given line with the toe, etc.

Farmers Market

This project is patterned after the famous Farmers Market in Los Angeles. One booth has nothing but a choice of several salads, another several kinds of sandwiches, another desserts, etc. Customers walk around with trays, buying whatever they want. Have card tables set up where they sit when they have completed buying their meal. If weather is favorable, this is grand for outdoors.

Musical Festival

Remember that participating brings even more pleasure than listening. Charge a small admission to a music-fest. You could start off with a medley of recorded music. That's merely a suggestion, but do have the first part be non-participating. This lets latecomers get settled and puts everyone in the proper mood.

Next, you might have a narrator explain the history of several songs and then have everyone join in singing them. Your local or state library can help you in your research.

After the song-stories, divide the room into sections for a musical quiz. The section with someone calling out the correct answer first is proclaimed winner. As a reward, they get to march up on the platform and sing! Here are suggested questions for the quiz:

1. What's the title of a song that has a color in it?
2. What song title has a time of day in it?
3. What is your favorite song?
4. What is the shortest song title you can think of?
5. What title has an animal in it?

You'll no doubt think of other questions. There are many answers for the above, of course. Here are suggested answers: 1. Blue Danube. 2. Three O'Clock in the Morning. 3. Everybody wins on this question! 4. He, Who. 5. Donkey Serenade.

After the winners have performed and marched back to their seats, conduct an old-fashioned sing. Be sure to have a peppy song leader and accompanist.

Book Fair

Books offer many possibilities. Reading clubs, book exchanges, literary luncheons and teas, discussion groups. A recent book fair for children was a big success.

There were no books sold. Instead, for five days children's books were displayed at different schools. The children attended in the afternoon and brought their parents in the evening. Authors of juvenile books were brought in from all over the area. They were ready to give autographs, short talks, and to mingle with the crowd.

The whole idea was to stimulate reading among youngsters. Local organizations were asked to send "hostesses" to greet and direct people.

You might use the same principle for a book fair. Perhaps you can arrange to buy books from a wholesaler at slightly above cost, and sell them. This is especially good if your town is small with no library.

Also good for a small group is an informal circle with the authors speaking. You could serve lunch afterward, and take a collection. If no writers are available, perhaps a teacher or a librarian could be the speaker. A good book review would tie in nicely.

A children's book fair is especially suitable for a PTA or any parents' group. The speaker could give pointers on how to select books for kids. Be sure to have a big display of books. You might want a representative from a local book store to help, and let him take orders for books.

Chapter Nine

FLOWER SHOW

A flower show can be the most attractive and interesting project your club sponsors. It is interesting and educational, and unites the community in a common cause.

Detailed planning is a **must.** The date should be left tentative until it is obvious when the flowers will be at their best. This date will vary slightly from year to year, depending on the weather.

Plan your show for flowers that grow best in your community. You may be able to have a daffodil show, while some other town boasts of lovely roses. You might prefer a show in the summer when you can have the biggest variety of flowers. Autumn shows are effective, too. A house plant show or Christmas floral decorations are other possibilities.

Committees should be chosen carefully and given definite duties. The number depends on the size of your group and how elaborate the show. The following can be a checklist of committees and duties:

1. Planning. In addition to selecting the date and type of show, this group can handle the publicity. No doubt local newspapers will be glad to co-operate. School art classes might make the posters.

The committee also sees to it that schedules are printed or mimeographed and widely circulated. Score cards for judges may be typewritten. The planning committee also can take care of ribbons or premiums for prizes.

2. Display. This group secures the showroom and properties. For best display along the walls, use ordinary tables from 30 to 36 inches wide. Build a shelf at the back edge with bricks and boards, approximately seven inches above the table. Placards can indicate the displays.

Be sure to leave wide aisles between the tables.

The display committee arranges the entries on the tables as soon as they're brought in and registered.

3. Registrar Committee. All entries should be checked in to this committee. Careful note should be made of name of entry and exhibitor. A label, bearing the code number, is then attached to the entry.

4. Judging Committee. This group obtains judges. Ask them well in advance of the approximate date. Then, when the date is final, let them know immediately.

It is best to have three judges. You might include a florist, an artist, and a woman famous for lovely table settings. The florist or flower club federation officers may have suggestions for suitable judges.

The judging committee sets up the schedule of classes to be shown. Naturally the schedule will be determined by the type of the show. You might like to divide yours into the following classifications:

Dept. 1—Flower arrangement

    Classes: In unusual containers, each listed as separate class. (Example: sugar bowl, pottery jug)

    Various flowers, each listed as a separate class. (If a "mixed" show. If not, various arrangements of the designated flower, in combinations with other flowers or foliage.)

Dept. 2—Specimen plants

Classes: The varieties are classified separately, whether they are all one flower, or varieties of many flowers. These are not judged on arrangement, but by a single stalk. Example: If a house plant show, varieties would include Blue Boy, etc., of African violets. If "mixed" show, include Bearded Iris, Hybrid Tea Rose, etc.

List these rules on printed schedules:

1. Amateurs only. (Note: You may include a professional class, but pros should not compete with amateurs.)

2. Plants must be grown by exhibitors unless otherwise specified.

3. No limit to number of classes entered, but only one entry to a class by a family. No exhibit can compete in more than one class.

4. Entry label must be attached to make the exhibit eligible.

5. All entries must be in place by **(time), (date),** at **(place).**

6. No one is allowed in the hall during judging except the judges.

7. Decision of the judges is final. They may disqualify any entry, or refuse to award premiums in any class not up to standard.

8. Entry fee is —— cents, payable upon registration.

In addition to the schedule, the judging committee should set up score cards for judging. (These are given to the planning committee who make copies for the judges. It is well to make a few extra copies.)

Be sure to include the following in the scoring: Flower arrangement—originality, balance and proportion, color combination, suitability of container, condition of bouquet. Speciman flowers—color, size of flower, stem length and stiffness, foliage, quality and condition of blossoms.

You might want to use the following score card, a favorite of several organizations:

Color harmony of all material	—25 points
Suitability of combination of material	—20 points
Distinction and originality	—25 points
Proportion and balance	—20 points
Conditions	—10 points
	100 points

Another judging scale for the flower arrangements is as follows:

Interpretation	—30 points
Distinction	—20 points
Color harmony	—20 points
Design	—20 points
Condition	—10 points
	100 points

Sometimes judges give as much as 35 points for imagination! In the case of complete table settings, you might want to include points for "suitability to occasion." (Example: Golden Wedding table.)

If you wish to include a program and refreshments, naturally you will need suitable committees.

Chapter Ten

HAPPY HOBBY DAY

Encourage people to display their valuable collections or a pet handicraft. Add to this natural interest of leisure-pleasure a bit of money-making and you have a project that is bound to be a success in your club. Plan on spending weeks on the affair. It takes lots of work, lots of planning—but both are easier when shared.

It is important to have plenty of committees. Be sure that they are composed of chairmen that know how to get things organized, and workers who really get things done. Give this committee-appointing a great deal of thought and put a woman on a job which is best suited to her.

Following is a list of committees. Naturally you will change it to suit the needs of your group, and the type affair you are going to undertake. Don't, for goodness sake, bite off more than you can chew. If the membership is low in numbers, keep the event simple. It can still be a success.

Committees:

Publicity	Program
Scouting	Refreshment
Pick-up	Award (optional)
Exhibit	Clean-up
Take-home	

Give the hobby show plenty of publicity. It will pay you to advertise in a local newspaper. Let children of the members help make posters. Ask ministers to announce the affair from the pulpit; ask teachers to tell children at school. Talk to the local editor. He may let one of your "writing" members do a feature story every few issues on the unusual hobbies, and of course the hobbyists, who are to be at the show. And remember, it is pretty hard to beat word-of-mouth when it comes to advertising something! Ask members to write their relatives all about it, too. Make it a regular "old home week" for your community.

The scouting committee will need the co-operation of everyone. If they hear even the tiniest rumor that someone within reasonable distance has a hobby, the committee should follow it up. Sometimes it takes a little tact to get a person to agree to "risk" their precious collections.

You may feel the need of asking all entrants to sign a release so your group won't be responsible for loss or breakage. Assure everybody the greatest care in the world will be taken, of course. Regardless of whether you ask for a signed release or not, you certainly should have blanks for the entrants to list the hobby, valuation (estimated), name, address and perhaps date when the hobby was started. You might set up a form something like this:

"I, _____, realizing the _____ club members will take the utmost care that nothing happens to my hobby, release them from responsibility of loss or breakage.

"My hobby is a salt and pepper shaker collection. I have 213 pairs and I value the collection at about $600.

Name and address."

The pick-up committee does just that. It can be combined with the take-home committee if you wish. Many entrants may prefer taking their own precious belongings themselves. But at any rate, your club should stand ready to haul the hobbies if necessary. Be sure and make lists! You want to be sure that every single hobby goes to its rightful home to roost.

The exhibit committee has a big job. Ask the owners to decorate their own booths and arrange their own exhibits, if they prefer. But this committee stands ready to do it for those who are not able.

You can be as simple or as elaborate in decorating booths as you wish. Be careful to make the decorations suit the hobby. Use quiet backgrounds for hobbies that make a splash by themselves, vivid surroundings for less impressive-looking exhibits.

If booths feature a handicraft, it adds interest to have the hobbyist demonstrate right there. The exhibit is bound to be surrounded with spectators most of the time. Do have a chair or two at each booth, one for the entrant, the other for a friend who wants to drop down and chat about the hobby.

Program committee should also have a group of good workers. You will find a suggested program at the end of these suggestions. Here again, you will want to adapt to suit your club's particular needs.

The award committee is optional. (You may decide giving awards, ribbons or prizes of any kind will cause more unkind thought than they will help the project!) Perhaps merchants will donate prizes for the cause. You could award the most unusual hobby, the most valuable collections, the biggest collection, the oldest hobby, the newest hobby, the oldest exhibitor, the youngest.

The clean-up committee gets the dirty work, of course. Although the take-home group returns any hobbies not taken home by owners, the clean-uppers make sure there is no mess left. This may mean the disrobing of booths, sweeping out, etc., especially if there is no janitor. If lunch is served, dishes come in this category.

As for refreshments, that too, is optional. A tea is a pretty good way to handle it at an event of this kind. Set up a tea table where spectators may drop by throughout the afternoon. If you wish, you can have a plate for a silver offering on the table. You may prefer a small admission to the entire show, however. If any hobbyists would like to sell their crafts, either ask for a small percentage or charge a fee to go into the club treasury.

Another way to make money is to set up one booth where you sell products such as greeting cards, your own cookbooks, fancywork or food donations. After all, your club's favorite pastime is making money, isn't it?

If you would like a full day's program, you may like to set up handicraft classes for the morning. Ask experts, home demonstration agents and others to teach and demonstrate. Or, if your club has been doing a series of such lessons, this hobby should make a wonderful climax or achievement day!

If this is a full day's program, you may want to sell a noon meal. Or, just for fun, make a potluck dinner of it. Your club can sell the coffee to add to the treasury.

Good luck to you! Here's hoping that you have a profitable and Happy Hobby Day.

Program:

Musical prelude

Invocation (may be used as a litany with the audience reading the underlined portion, if you use printed or mimeographed programs).

"Oh, God, giver of all good things,
We thank Thee.
For the joy of creating,
We thank Thee.
For today's modern equipment that makes leisure time
activity possible.
Father, we thank Thee.
For the broadening of our horizons through our hobbies,
For the stimulating, interesting mother, wife and citizen
each of us can be from such leisure time activities,
For the joy of creating, as we see it,
Each in our own way,
Father, we thank Thee.   Amen."

Instrumental music
Solo—(by someone whose hobby is music)
Reading—(by someone whose hobby is writing or reciting
poetry or monologues)
Music
Talk—"There's a hobby at our house" (by a woman whose
family enjoys an interesting hobby together)
Skit—"Treasures of My Leisure" (soloist and other music
groups are hidden behind the stage unless otherwise
indicated. Keep the background music—probably a
piano—soft).

READER: A hobby-horse is said to be a toy horse on which
one rides and rides without getting anywhere. But we don't
really believe that—or we wouldn't be here today. We know
sometimes we really **do** get somewhere when we ride a hobby-
horse, as we say. We derive much pleasure from our handicrafts. The word "craft" is an old Teutonic word meaning
strength.

There is strength and value in a hobby. All work and no play makes Jill a dull wife and mother. Cooking, laundry, chores—all these are necessary to your family's welfare and happiness. But it is also important that you keep your identity as an individual—a stimulating, creative person. And that's where a hobby comes in!

When you're physically tired, working on your pet pastime can be actually restful. Perhaps after the children are tucked into bed, you can relax with your project. Evening hours are often favorites for hobbies. (Background music — "In the Gloaming.")

READER: Perhaps, though, your favorite hobby is enjoying some sport with your husband.

(Two or three women enter, dressed in jeans, shirt and baseball cap, singing, "Take Me Out to the Ball Game." They exit quickly.)

READER: Or you may prefer a less strenuous pastime. For example, you may like to read or study.

(Musical background—"School Days.")

READER: Many women enjoy painting such things as a lovely woodland scene. A woman enters. She may be one of those who wore jeans—and sets up an easel. She pretends to paint as the soloist sings, "There's a Long, Long Trail," and exits.

READER: Some women we know sew because they think they must; others sew because they think it it fun. Enter four women in house dresses. One has a large pair of shears which she clicks in time to the music. Another carries a length of fabric; another a hem-marker. The fourth has something such as a pin cushion. They sing the following through together once, then as a round:

(Tune—"Row Your Boat.")
Sew, sew, sew a seam
Quickly by machine.
Merrily, merrily, merrily, merrily,
Make things like a dream!

READER: You may like knitting, embroidery, textile painting or rug making. What does it matter, just so **you** enjoy it? One woman says when she is dead-tired from housework, it rests her to dance!

(Musical background—"The Waltz You Saved for Me.")

READER: No doubt you've heard the verse by Owen Meredith:

"Ye may live without poetry, music and art;
We may live without conscience, and live without heart;
We may live without friends,
We may live without looks;
But civilized men cannot live without cooks!"

Some women make a satisfying hobby of cooking. And that's one hobby to which families certainly don't object!

(Soloist sings, "If I knew You Were Comin', Ida' Baked a Cake," or group sings, "Shortnin' Bread.")

READER: Hobbies differ in the amount of contentment they give us. Usually we get out of them just what we put into them. One of the most satisfying pastimes is to be in our place in church every Sunday.

(Group sings, "Little Brown Church in the Vale.")

READER: Sometimes our leisure-time activities bring others pleasure, too. Probably this is as true of music as any other.

(Soloist steps out in sight and sings any solo she does exceptionally well. "The Lost Chord" would be lovely.)

You can conclude the program with a benediction, or announcing awards if any were given. Also, you may want to give acknowledgements, thank committees and co-operation of hobbyists, merchants, or any others who had a part in making the hobby show a success.

Chapter Eleven

BAZAARS

As the place where you hold the bazaar helps determine what type it will be, decide on a location first. For a big community affair, you may want to use the park where you can set up many open air booths. The school athletic field is another possibility. Or hire a hall or gym for a big indoor fair. You can use someone's lawn for a smaller project.

A street fair is popular but don't forget to get permission from city authorities.

When you set the date, don't try to compete with a similar affair to be given within a few weeks. Don't attempt to rival a carnival, circus, or other commercial event.

Publicity

You must stir up enthusiasm beforehand. You do want a good attendance whether it is from curiosity, loyalty, or hunting entertainment. The work of the publicity committee begins the minute the plans are made!

If possible, give the names and pictures of all bazaar committee members. Name the place where the fair will be held, and the date. Other hints on publicity are given in another chapter.

Merchandising

This is important for a bazaar. Some of the items could be homemade. They include sewing and embroidery, crocheting and knitting, cakes and jellies. But don't overlook the possibility of buying in quantity at wholesale prices, or at a discount. Just be sure you are buying a popular item before stocking it in quantity. You don't want a lot of leftovers.

You can probably count on a few donations from local merchants, too, unless they've been solicited extensively already.

Soliciting

Be sure each member is asked to donate something. There's bound to be someone hurt if left out. Also, be careful no one is asked several times over—that can be even worse!

Decide if people are to be asked for specific items or given their choice. Perhaps you should at least give them an idea of the items you need most. Some may even prefer to give money, which is always helpful! It goes without saying that the solicitors must be tactful.

Collectors

These probably should be young, energetic women with cars. Collecting is quite a chore. A list is essential. Mrs. Nelson isn't going to want to make aprons that aren't called for! Probably one collector should be assigned to food, another to needlework, and so on.

One group accumulates bazaar items all during the year. Each member takes an article, either purchased or handmade, to the meeting nearest her birthday anniversary. A chairman stores the items until bazaar time.

Don't overlook the possibility of donations by merchants for the publicity it gives them. Even donated work for the lighting can be credited to the electrician in news stories and placards.

Marking Committee

These committee members should put prices on the articles as soon as they are delivered. They'll need to know values and the type customer expected.

Three things determine the price you should charge for handwork: cost of material, amount of work, and demand. You should also consider the usual price charged for such handwork in your community.

General Suggestions

Booths can be arranged facing one another in two rows, street fair fashion. Simply lay planks on saw-horses, dividing

Booths may be simply planks on saw horses. Or you can build a foundation, such as one of these shown. Uprights may be nailed to the four corners and cross pieces fastened between them (c). Adding a roof effect (b) is more substantial, gives you more elaborate decorating possibilities.

Heavy wires, laths, or bamboo strips may be fastened from front corners to opposite back corners and fastened where they cross (a). Bamboo or wire arches can be used across the front or back.

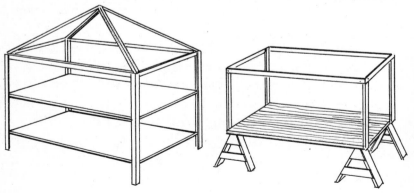

the space off into cubicles by temporary partitions. Or you can build booths as individual units. (See Fig. 1 and Fig. 2.) Deco-

rations such as a mobile (see Fig. 3 and Fig. 4, Page 116) add a festive air.

Don't despair if your bazaar is so small you can't have booths. You can still display your goods so it will look its very best and attract attention. You might want to line the walls with old sheets and pin the handwork to them. Label everything plainly with price tags. One advantage of a small affair is the friendly hospitality that prevails. Make every customer feel welcome!

Food bars are popular at bazaars, particularly if you don't plan to sell a full meal. You might set up a pie bar, with coffee; a cake bar; homemade candy, etc.

And how about a household help booth? Most women will spend money to lighten their chores. You can offer dust cloths, clothespin bags, potholders, table mats, cleaning pads, etc.

Add a special touch to common things to increase their sales appeal. For example, a red and white potholder, a red and white dish cloth and a white dish towel with a bright red appliqued apple would probably sell separately. But why not make a gift package of them? Wrap them all in cellophane, plastic or Saran wrap. Add some bright ribbon and a gay sticker and you'll have a nice gift.

Likewise, a box of plain stationery has little appeal. Take

the same box, add a colored blotter and a small bottle of matching ink.

Themes

A theme helps any bazaar and is wonderful for the publicity committee. An attendant in costume makes a good newspaper photo. Once you choose a theme, you'll be amazed how interesting it is to work out ideas that tie in.

For example, set up booths in a complete circle, with the attendants inside the circle. Then have the men arrange a canopy top, and lo! you have a merry-go-round or carousel.

Many other themes are given here. Even the smallest bazaar can be planned around a central theme. Just do it on a smaller scale. You'll find that your bazaar has never been as enjoyable to plan as when you work out a theme of your very own!

Place and Show

This is a do-it-yourself age. Advertise your bazaar as a place where the customer can watch it being done! Ever notice that in a dime store or at a fair, the crowds are around the woman showing **how** she made the rugs or whatever product is displayed?

A booth of handicrafts such as textile painting could have a woman sitting nearby actually doing some designs. Some people have never even seen crocheting done! The elderly woman who tires easily will be happy to sit and crochet as people come to buy.

Of course the demonstrators should be willing to answer questions. There are many popular crafts that would make fascinating demonstrations.

Little Jewel

Advertise that if customers come, they may find a "little jewel" of a bargain! Decorate booths in appropriate color, using crepe paper. The emerald booth could be for plants in their natural greenery. The diamond can be all white, and feature articles for the bride. However, the wares need not be tied in with the color used.

Attendants of each booth wear appropriate colors. Sell chances on "jewels"—costume jewelry. (That is, if your organization is not opposed to lottery.)

Winter Wonderland

Many bazaars are given just before the holiday season. Take advantage of winter weather by using it as your theme. You can make the windows look frosted over by putting washing powder suds on them. Hang white paper icicles from the ceiling. Arrange tree boughs around the room with cotton and artificial snow on them. Decorate all the booths in white and be generous with the use of artificial snow. (Salt looks frosty, too.)

Calendar

Decorate booths to represent months. If you don't have twelve booths, you might use alternating months. Or you might feature those with holidays, and naturally the easiest to decorate.

Have Father Time roaming around, selling "grabs." He should wear a tall hat, a beard, and carry a scythe.

Circus Bazaar

Actual tickets (as to a circus) can be sold. Ticket takers, hostesses, and attendants may be dressed as clowns or other circus characters.

Decorate the room as the Midway. Be lavish with the use of balloons and pennants. Booths are each decorated with awnings to look like the small tents.

Arrange a canvas canopy at one end of the hall for the Big Tent, the dining space. Here you can sell supper. In addition,

A Circus Bazaar is fun to plan and decorate.

you might want booths with pink lemonade, cotton candy, and ice cream cones for those not wanting a complete meal.

Harmonious Bazaar

Decorate each booth to represent a song title. Sell chances to guess the title at each booth for a penny each. At the end of the bazaar, announce the winner. Gixe inexpensive prizes.

TV Bazaar

The hall is a television studio! Each booth is a different "set," with a room background. Rig up some imitation television cameras to set about the room. Have lots of lights set up, too.

Post placards here and there with such signs as: Quiet, Please; Control Room; On the Air; Studio One, etc. You might number each booth as Studio One, Studio Two, and so on.

Set up a table with a big sign, INFORMATION. Be sure the attendant is well informed on what is featured at each booth, cost of articles, and other details.

Rainbow Bazaar

Each booth is decorated as one of the colors of the rainbow. At one end of the hall, build an imitation rainbow with a pot of gold at one end. This is the grab bag, for which you sell chances to grab. Articles are small and wrapped in gold foil. Or you can fill the pot with gold-foil wrapped discs and sell chances on how many are in the pot.

Garden Bazaar

Cover walls with lattice and crepe paper or real flowers. Have card tables at one end where refreshments are served. Each booth can be almost like a flower bower or stall. Arrange watering pots and other garden tools around for atmosphere.

Fill a wishing well with inexpensive items for a grab bag. A wheelbarrow can hold other small packages that people buy, sight unseen.

All Seasons

You'll have only four main booths for this. Decorate each to represent Spring, Summer, Fall, or Winter. If you serve a meal, you might do it at four tables and use a seasonal centerpiece on each. Perhaps the guests might even sit at the table for the season in which their birthday falls.

Indian Village

Decorate booths to look like teepees. Attendants wear Indian costumes. You may even want one booth of Indian jewelry. Perhaps you can also have a booth of ceramics, with some of Indian design. This is especially good if your club has been sponsoring a ceramic workshop or class.

Baskets, too, go along with this theme. And of course you'll have the usual needlework and regular booths. The attendants and decorations carry out the theme.

Holiday Bazaar

Decorate the booths to represent the different holidays. The Halloween can be in orange and black with pumpkins, black cats, and all the usual symbols. You'll be able to think of decorations for all the holidays. Try to sell items in keeping with each booth's theme as much as possible.

Library Bazaar

This is similar to the song-title booths. Instead, use titles of well-known books. Attendants can be dressed like the heroines. You can also have guessing of their names, if you wish.

Set up one booth of used books in good condition. Often families have juveniles after the children are grown, or a novel that's been read and no longer wanted.

Around the World

You might decorate each booth to represent a different country. Attendants can be dressed in suitable costume.

Mother Goose Land

This theme is fun! Decorate each booth to represent one of the Mother Goose verses. The chairman, who mingles about among the customers, can be Mother Goose herself!

Shakespearean

Plan booths for the different plays. Posters can be in old English, with scenes appropriate for the time. Attendants wear costumes. Ophelia, with a white gown and sash at the waist, wears a crown of leaves and flowers. She presides at the plant and flower stand. The King and Queen of fairies can be at the Midsummer Night's Dream booth. For a humorous touch, let Lady MacBeth sell household cleansers and spot removers! You'll have fun thinking of others.

This is especially good for a cultural group where people are most familiar with Shakespeare's characters.

The Shakespearean tea, mentioned in another chapter (Teas), could be held the same day as this fair, with a slight charge or silver offering.

Pioneer Bazaar

Those at booths, those selling tickets, and all workers should be in overalls or aprons. The girls wear sunbonnets. Decorations are in keeping, too, of course. Used old-fashioned pictures, kerosene lamps, etc.

A toy stall might feature farm animals. An old-fashioned well hides a lemonade stand! Or the well could be used for the "fishing pond."

The possibilities are limited only by your space and the amount of donations. A good old "country supper" can be sold, too.

A Make-Believe Bazaar

This is particularly good during the busy holiday season. Have notices typed, printed or mimeographed and sent to all the members. Try to keep the project a secret, except for the committee, until the notices are sent out. Mail them all at once so they'll all be received at the same time.

"Dear Member:

Are you so busy you're practically going in circles? So is everyone else! The _____ Club is sponsoring a Make-Believe Bazaar. This is how it works: read the following statements, fill in the blanks, and give the total amount of money to the treasurer. We suggest you do it before Christmas. You'll no doubt have enough post-holiday bills without any additional expense!

1. Amount of money I would spend on material to make-up for a bazaar _____.

2. Number of hours it would take me to make the article(s) _____. Amount of pay I would expect for that many hours work _____.

3. Expense for transportation of articles to bazaar _____. Transportation of my family to the bazaar _____. Transportation to any committee meetings I might attend _____. Total transportation _____.

4. Amount of money I would spend buying things I don't especially want _____.

5. Amount I might spend for things I do want _____.

6. Cost of food I would donate to the bazaar supper _____

7. Hours of time in preparing the food, or serving it _____ Amount that much time is worth _____.

8. Amount I would spend for my family's meals at the bazaar _____.

9. My "thank you" offering for getting out of all this work _____."

Of course, you can adapt the above to suit the particular features of your usual bazaar.

Extra Money at Bazaars

It's quantity in small amounts that makes much of the profit at a bazaar. People will spend a dime here, a quarter there, where they'll hesitate to spend several dollars. So plan extra attractions, such as grab bags. We give you some variations for grab bags. Items may be purchased or donated.

Mobile Grab

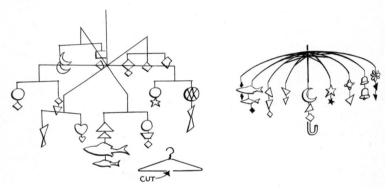

Fig. 3. Mobile made from coat hangers.

Fig. 4. Mobile made from an umbrella.

Make a mobile like Fig. 3 or Fig. 4. Hang small prizes on it.

Theme Grab

If your bazaar is built around a special theme, plan a grab bag that is appropriate. It isn't difficult to think of something suitable.

The Lady With the Hundred Pockets

Ask one of your members to dress in a hoopskirt or an old-fashioned dress. She wears a bonnet and carries an umbrella. In her dress are many pockets, sewed on for the occasion, in which little prizes are hidden.

The child pays his dime and gets to select the pocket. The "old lady" then gives him the gift hidden there.

Peachy Grab Bag

Wrap small articles in peach-colored crepe paper and tie to a real tree branch potted in sand. Sell the "peaches" for a dime each.

Buried Treasure

A bazaar held in a school gym featured buried treasure. The "treasures" were found in the sand of the kindergarten sand table, borrowed for the occasion. The grabs sold for a nickel each—for children only. They loved hunting in the sand for their buys.

Grand March

Try a grand march for prizes. Mark off a large square with fifteen or twenty numbered squares around the edge. Have a barker go through the crowd, selling chances for a dime each. When you've sold as many chances as squares, start the music. Contestants march around the circle several times. Suddenly stop the music and draw a number. Person standing on the square with that number is the winner.

You can go through all sorts of maneuvers before you stop the music, and of course the contestants follow you. Have as many grand marches, stopping the music each time, as you have prizes.

Fortune Telling

This usually can be done with home talent and is bound to draw a crowd. Everybody has a little natural curiosity about his future! Use the usual atmosphere—a mysterious curtain, a costumed fortune teller, perhaps a crystal ball. Or the gypsy can read palms.

Check at your city or state library for information on palm reading. There have been a number of articles written on the subject.

Bazaar Items

Ask your members, "What can you make, or have someone make, for us to sell?" Sometimes the club pays for the materials and the members donate their time to make them.

In one club, a member worked at a garment factory. She was able to get small remnants free. The club worked on quilts, patchwork aprons, and other articles made from the scraps, at meetings. Some of the women took the scraps home to work on between times.

Felt Novelties

They're quickly made and usually sell. Try stuffed toys, slippers, beanies, belts, coin purses, earrings. And felt skirts are popular now.

A beautiful holiday cloth is made of red or green felt. Work out an appropriate design for sequins and felt cutouts.

You can use the same idea for an "apron" to put around the Christmas tree. Cut felt in a huge circle with a hole in the middle. Cut the circle in two at one side only. This is for inserting the tree trunk into the center hole. The apron lies flat on the floor. It makes a pretty background for piling Christmas presents, and for catching pine needles.

Make red felt Christmas stockings and sew a bell on the toe. These socks can be personalized with the name of the child the sock is being purchased for.

Christmas Cards

These are nice if you have local scenes reproduced. (Your city park in winter, the church, main street, etc.) Your local printer can add, "Greetings from Noel Center" or the name of your town.

Christmas Tags and Name Cards

One organization made effective name cards from old Christmas cards. You'll be surprised what attractive shapes and effects you can get. Package them in little cellophane envelopes such as stamp collectors use.

Fringed Luncheon Sets

They're pretty, and so quick! The secret is in the lovely color combinations you work out. Be sure to machine-stitch before raveling the edges.

Crayon Aprons

Make a cobbler type apron for little girls. Instead of the usual wide pockets across the bottom, stitch narrow vertical pockets. Each is just the size to hold a colored crayon. Embroider a gay design to suggest "coloring."

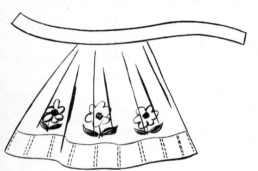

Crayon Cobbler Apron is a good seller. Make the same as any apron for a little girl, but add a wide band across bottom. The band has stitched, narrow pockets just big enough for slipping in the crayons.

A boy's carpenter apron can be made the same way. If you add the toy tools, or the crayons, up the price.

Artificial Corsages

Pretty, if skillfully done. Perhaps someone in your club has the knack.

Scrappy Favorites

Solicit scraps and remnants ahead of time from other church groups, relatives, and friends. Don't turn up your nose at a bit of lace, an unusual button, or anything! Then just see how many things you can make. You might even give a prize for the most unusual creation.

Designing and making the articles can be done after the business session of several meetings before the bazaar. Here are ideas for scraps: novel potholders, stuffed toys, bean bags, doll clothes, patchwork aprons, shopping bags and silverware kits. What can you come up with?

Homemade Jams and Jellies

This takes beforehand work. Ask the women to make a few extra jars during their jelly-making season.

Winter Bouquets

Don't tackle this unless you have a really artistic member. She can use seed pods, grasses, and pine cones. Branches are cleaned and dried, left natural, or dipped in white, silver, or green. Powders or sprays blown on are easy. Art or paint stores may be able to give instructions.

It's a good idea to have sample bouquets for taking orders.

Mother-Daughter Sets

This is a popular feature. There's a definite appeal about "the same thing in miniature." Make a set of aprons, pinafores, nighties, or whatever you wish. If they don't sell as a set, you can always price them individually.

Wood Carving

Wooden plaques, with tots' favorite designs, are good if someone is handy. And what little girl wouldn't love a doll-house? Perhaps there's a woodcarver in a member's family.

Swedish Weaving

A lovely stitch, especially appropriate for guest towels, luncheon sets, dainty aprons. Swedish weaving goes faster than many embroidery stitches.

Textile Painting

This sells, if done skillfully. Perhaps there has been a textile painting class in your group. Or a ceramics class? Sell the results!

Chapter Twelve

HOME TALENT PLAYS
AND PROGRAMS

A home talent play is usually a real money-maker. It takes lots of time because of rehearsals. But it usually turns out that the actors have a wonderful time at play-practice and are almost sorry when it is over!

Plan to spend at least two or three weeks preparing for the simplest one-act play, and have rehearsals every week. The lines should be memorized as early as possible. It is hard to work on the action and try to remember a line at the same time.

First, select a director. If he is a professional, so much the better. Perhaps you know a retired school teacher who formerly directed plays. Or maybe one of your members was quite active in a civic theater group in another city. Think hard—you'll probably find someone with experience in this field.

The first job of the director is to select a play. He may want the help of a committee, particularly if he isn't too familiar with your group. Choose a play easy to stage, with not many players. A comedy usually goes over best. Real drama is difficult to portray by amateurs. At any rate, the play should have plenty of action, suspense, conflict, and a good climax. Select it according to the group's ability and avoid "the same old thing." Choose a play that is not too long nor too involved.

When the play has been chosen, the director will want to read and re-read it. This gives him an idea about how he wants the players to present it.

Try a home-talent play for fun and profit.

Next, comes the casting. Here again the director may ask for a little help if he doesn't know your members well. He might even want to conduct "readings" or try-outs. Of course the main characters should be chosen first, as they are usually the biggest problems. However, many times a lesser character steals the show!

You'll probably want a committee to see about designing the "sets." Perhaps a carpenter will be necessary, unless you can contrive appropriate settings from whatever is at hand. This same committee is responsible for changing sets, if more than one is used, during the play.

Giving a historical play? Special costumes may be necessary with a committee responsible. If the usual clothing is worn, the actors can be responsible for seeing about their own costumes.

Properties usually can be collected from among the townspeople. The committee should have a complete list, including smaller props such as a water pitcher, etc. This committee not only collects the props, but sees to getting them back. Who can blame a family for refusing to loan an armchair that may not be returned for several weeks after the play is over?

How to Put On Make-up

Make-up is slightly different for the stage than for the street. The amount is determined by the brightness of the lights used. The more light, the more make-up. Characters are apt to look pasty-faced and washed out unless they have extra color.

You'll need theatrical cold cream, grease paint or base, medium cream rouge, medium lipstick (women can wear their own), liners of dark brown and black, blue and green eye shadow, brunette and juvenile powder. You should also have toothpicks, cleansing tissues, a large roll of cotton, and a baby brush. You can order supplies from the publishers of this book.

Apply eye shadow to upper lid. Use liner to make a line closer to upper edge of the eyelid following to outer corner. Do the same below the lower lid, starting in the center of the lid and drawing line to outer corner. Apply a dot of rouge with a toothpick to inner corner of each eye.

Here is probably the best order for putting on stage make-up:

1. Cold-cream the face and neck thoroughly. This protects the skin and removes old make-up—which **must** be done.

2. Apply the base. Most people look best with Juvenile blended with a little Robust or yellow. Instructions that come with stage make-up should give variations for men, extreme blondes, etc. Blend the base on smoothly and carefully.

3. Apply rouge. Make a few dots on each cheek. Blend gently in toward the nose and out toward the top of the ear. Run your rouged finger under the eyebrow. Be careful not to get any on the eyelids.

4. Apply eye shadow to upper lid. Use liner to make a line closer to upper edge of the eyelid following to outer corner. Do the same below the lower lid, starting in the center of the lid and drawing line to outer corner. Apply a dot of rouge with a toothpick to the inner corner of each eye.

5. Follow natural browline with eyebrow pencil or liner.

6. Lipstick can be applied with lipstick brush or from the tube.

7. Powder should be a shade lighter than the base, but the same tone. Press powder into the skin and dust off with a soft brush. Powder all exposed parts of the body.

Now you're ready for the production. There's no business like show business, so on with the show!

What to Present

Orchestra

Perhaps you have half a dozen women in your club who can play a musical instrument. That's all you need! It's better not to start with a large group, anyway, until the project is well under way. Just be sure those who are participating are really interested and willing to spend the hours necessary for practice.

Essential instruments are piano, violin, clarinet and trumpet. As you grow, you'll want to add flute, saxophones, string bass, trombone, cello, with perhaps oboe, French and alto horns, and drums even later. Of course the main requirement for an orchestra is good strings.

Perhaps a high school music teacher will be glad to help you out. One of your own musicians might learn to direct, with a little professional help for a time or two.

As soon as you're good enough, you can start playing in public with an admission charge. Don't expect much money until the orchestra has been in full swing about a year. In the meantime, you might charge each musician a small fee to join the orchestra.

Novelty Groups

Many women's clubs get a great kick out of a "kitchen band." Their instruments are utensils, a piano, and "kazoos." Kazoos are little humming tune-makers; you can buy them at the dime store. Disguise them with kitchen utensils, such as a meat grinder! The leader directs with a wooden spoon. Play familiar tunes that the women know well.

Play at various public functions for a small fee. Or pass the hat for an offering.

The women should wear uniforms of some type, perhaps kitchen aprons.

In one such band, each player took the name of a well-known TV personality and dressed accordingly. The leader introduced them and they responded as the star would. Listen carefully to television programs for phrases that the actors use again and again. To vary, have the players sing part of the time.

Minstrel Shows

An old-time minstrel show is always popular. Your best bet is to get a director and he should have a book on the subject.

The greatest appeal of the minstrel is the fact that jokes, skits, and stunts mention local people and events. You can build the show around a theme such as a Barn Dance, Gay Nineties, County Fair, or any such subjects. Begin filling in appropriate numbers of acts, keeping in mind the available talent, and your plans are under way!

Most minstrel shows feature a chorus, dancers, jokes and songs by the "interlocutor" and the "end men." Then the second part of the show is known as the "olio," a series of humorous stunts. You can use current events, history, jokes, etc. With a little twist and a few local names, they become stunts. They shouldn't be stiff and letter-perfect but have the effect of being spontaneous. Even so, better rehearse a time or two to make them move along smoothly.

The show must be kept moving at all times. Avoid delays in entrances and exits. Encourage the actors to over-act to add to the humor.

As stated before, you definitely should have a director and a book of instructions for a good minstrel show.

Play Rings

Several clubs in one county prepared plays. Then they changed nights with one another until each play had been shown in each neighborhood. In each case, the home group handles all the arrangements and sells the tickets. Proceeds are divided with the visiting group. This gives each community a season of entertainment and nets a nice profit.

Elimination Plays

In another county, several clubs worked up plays for their own community. After the plays had been given once, the groups then competed, two by two, in an elimination contest. Of course there was great rivalry and competition to see which club would give the winning play. Naturally, ticket sales were high.

Home Talent Night

In an Eastern church, a Home Talent Night is the highlight of each year. It includes such things as beginning piano pupils' first solos, duets, poems, readings, instrumental music. There is no idea of showing off the kids, but the slight admission really helps the church funds. Your club might like to try it.

All that's needed is one rehearsal with the full cast. People have fun at home working out their own numbers, costuming and practicing.

1. Line up the talent. Announce in the church bulletin and ask anyone interested to report to the committee. Remember, this may not bring them all out. Some people like to be coaxed!

2. Aim for variety. Suggest ideas when people can't think of what to do. You won't want a whole evening of recitations, for example. Boys might prefer magic tricks, Indian club exercises, and similar stunts. It would be grand if there's a one-family band or chorus in town.

3. If there is danger of the program getting too long, perhaps several persons can group together. They would not necessarily have to be in the same family. Such a group could do a skit, or one could play the piano while the others go into their act.

4. Vary the approach, too. Perhaps you can use the TV program gimmick. Have a master of ceremonies at one side. He has the program, and informally gives a few words about each number.

The young actors can enter from the opposite side of the platform where the emcee sits. You should have an assistant to usher each act into place at its turn. The assistant could even escort the youngsters clear out to the emcee. Getting across the stage is sometimes the hardest part for amateurs.

The master of ceremonies can chat with each a minute or two. Ask what grade he is in, and other things. End up with, "What are you going to do for us?" The child is relaxed by then, and in this way he announces his own number.

The assistant has the next number ready as soon as one goes out. No stage curtain is necessary.

Puppet Shows

Puppets and marionette shows returned with television. Adults as well as children like to watch them, and even want to learn to make and manipulate them.

Your club might start up a little theater. The women will get a big kick out of making the stage, puppets, and working up shows. It's usually not hard to sell tickets to a show of this kind.

How to Make Puppets

Making puppets and marionettes is largely a matter of experimenting. We give you four methods here:

1. You can make heads of modeling clay. Then comes a plaster of Paris cast into which plastic wood is pressed. This gives a hollow head so the puppets can have open eyes and mouth. Bodies generally are made of wood, as are arms and legs.

The hardest part may be in getting the eyes and mouth to fit so they'll operate smoothly. The final touch is painting the puppets, and making their clothes.

2. Buy small dolls at the dime store. Remove their heads and hands. Make a muslin "mitten" with two fingers, and a hole at the top. Sew the hole around the doll head, and each "finger" hole around a doll hand. The bottom of the mitten is left open and fits over your own hand.

You insert a thumb in one of the puppet's "arms," and your little finger in the other. The other three fingers of your hand are inserted into the doll's empty head. Or it may be more convenient for you to place the index finger in the head, the middle finger in one arm, and the thumb in the other arm.

Now, see how you can make the puppet's arms and head move? This is the simplest kind of puppet.

3. You can make heads from muslin. Dye a pillow case or

part of an old sheet a flesh color. Cut two profiles for each character. Set the sewing machine to the shortest stitch and sew just as close to the edge as possible. Turn, and with a fine, dull-pointed stick press out the seams.

Stuff the head firmly with cotton. Then shape the face so it will look natural. Push a place up through the center of the inside of the head. This is where your index finger fits so you can move the head. Do not stuff the neck, but leave it to sew to the costume. Paint features on the face with enamel paint.

Hands can be made in the same way as the head.

4. Marionettes can be made with a crepe paper clay. It is easy to mold and light in weight. The following recipe should be enough for two marionettes.

Cut two folds of flesh-colored crepe paper into a bowl, in small confetti-like pieces. Cover with two cups of water and let stand a few hours. Drain off the excess water and add one cup flour and two tablespoons of salt. Mix together with your fingers and knead until you get a clay-like consistency.

To make the head, you'll need a tube. You can make it out of a 4-by-3-inch piece of lightweight cardboard. Build up around this tube with the crepe paper clay until you have a head-shape. Leave about one-half inch of the tube showing for the neck (Fig. A).

Form features by adding more crepe paper clay. You can make fine details with an ice pick.

Arms and legs are made the same way, except the tubes are smaller. Cut two 2½-inch pieces of the cardboard and roll for tubes (for arms). Overlap ends about a half-inch and fasten with cellulose tape. Fill these tubes solidly with crepe paper clay. At the end of each tube, use more clay to make hands. (You can omit fingers—make the hand like a mitten.) See Fig. B.

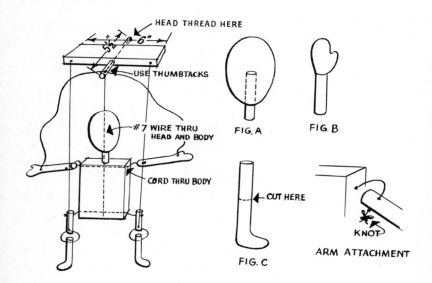

How to make a puppet (Type 4).

The legs are made the same, but you'll need to make the tubes from two pieces 2½ by 4½ inches. Make a clay shoe. When the leg is dry, remove the cardboard tubes. Cut the leg in two at the point where a knee would be. Fig. C.

The body is a small box. Fill the bottom part with the clay.

Pack it in firmly and smooth off the top. Dry the body, arms and legs in a sunny place. It usually takes two or three days. The tubes can be peeled off when the pieces are nearly dry. Be sure each is thoroughly dry before painting.

Make holes in the box with an ice pick or awl. Fasten all the parts to the body with thread. You'll also need threads long enough to manipulate the marionette from above. A "crutch" at the top makes it easier. (See Fig. D.)

Add yarn or crepe paper fringe for hair. Paint on features, shoes, etc. You can add a coat of clear shellac to the whole marionette. Make clothes from remnants.

The crutch, which controls actions of the marionette, is made of wood. Holes are drilled. Use carpet thread (rub with beeswax so it won't knot or tangle). Four strings are used— one to each leg, one to head, and one controls the arms. (See Fig. D.)

Check at your city or state library for instruction books if you have difficulty making puppets or marionettes.

Action!

Most puppeteers work behind a curtain. However, one successful marionette team works in plain sight of the audience. They wear black uniforms with long black sleeves and gloves. When the spotlights are on the puppets, you can scarcely see the operators. And adults get a kick out of watching "how it's done."

The puppet show stage is usually made quite high. This permits the operator to hide in a curtained space underneath. The puppets are inserted on the hands of the operator. One person can handle two puppets at a time if he has an assistant to take each puppet off his hand and put on another when a new character goes on stage. However, it's easier to have two operators.

Regardless of whether you use marionettes or puppets, you'll need to do a great deal of practice. Try to keep movements smooth, not jerky. There are even schools of training for puppetry, if any of your members get **that** interested in the project.

It is impossible to give a script here as it depends on what type of show you want to give. Here's hoping your club has a clever script writer!

Your play can be purely nonsense, teach a lesson in a humorous way, or present a Bible story. Think of the audience you expect and plan something you are sure they will enjoy. A few successful performances, and everyone will be wanting tickets!

Be sure to tape the script to the inside of the booth. A puppet show has the advantage that you don't have to memorize the lines. You can use only the operator's voices, or add others—if you can find a place to hide other speakers!

The instructions as given here merely touch on the great field of puppetry. If your group becomes really interested, try to find a professional instructor. And, as mentioned before, your library should have helpful material.

Chapter Thirteen

TRACK-AN-ACT PROGRAM

Amateur shows are popular. Favorite radio and TV programs prove that. Give a community amateur show for a natural money-maker. Better still, give it a new slant for added interest.

Here is how a Track-an-Act program works. First, choose your committee. Each member is to "track down" someone in the community who can contribute a number for your program. Suggest that a variety of numbers be presented. The committee may want to meet and compare notes to be sure they don't have in mind talent that would mean an entire evening of hill-billy music, for example.

Select a good master of ceremonies. He may find himself on the spot once in awhile and have to do a little ad-libbing.

The best part of this program is that no rehearsal is necessary. Each individual is responsible for his own number. It is more fun to participants if they do not see the script at all. Then the master of ceremonies' remarks come as a complete surprise.

It is to be understood that the script is to be adapted to the group and the circumstances. Use local names if you are sure they are "good sports."

To make that money we mentioned, charge a small admission. Or sell votes. Contestant who has most votes in his name is winner of the show.

Arrange the stage to resemble a television studio. (Study the picture of one for ideas.) Probably you will want a suspended "boom" hanging from the ceiling. Add a few wires, an old camera on a tripod, floor lamps and other props.

CHARACTERS:

Cracker Jack—wears suit coat or sports jacket, false moustache and big bow tie. Very breezy; fair "barker" type. If necessary, dress a woman for the part.

Mr. Cracker Jack is announcer for the "Track-an-Act Program."

Henry J. Henry—reads commercials. Try to have this character the exact opposite of Cracker Jack. If one is lean, the other fat or vice versa. May be a woman.

Ushers—may be teen-age girls.

Trackers—the committee members. As written, there are five women. Change to suit your purpose.

Actors: Script includes a married man, one married woman, teen-age girl, a bachelor or widower, and a child. This set-up will have to be changed to suit whatever acts are presented. (Trackers must tell their "finds" to Cracker Jack beforehand to allow him to change his script to suit the character of performers.)

(Enter Cracker Jack with wide "toothpaste" grin. Holds arms above head as to signal camera men.)

JACK: Hell-o, hell-o, everybody. This is your old palsy-walsy, Cracker Jack, ready to bring you the top-flight entertainers of all time.

HENRY: (Rushes in.) All time, you say? The big news of all time is Bleep, the washday habit. Bleep is the successor of Bloop, as Bloop has been bought out by Bleep, manufacturer of the news in soap (hiccups). If Bloop felt Bleep was good enough to buy Bloop, then Bleep should be good enough for you! Bloop-Bleep is the full name, ladies. But we fondly call it by its nickname, Bleep. Buy a carton tomorrow! (Hiccups.)

JACK: Yes, ladies, your Track-an-Act show is being sponsored by Bleep, the washday habit. (In a stage whisper to Henry: "Why don't you do something about those hiccups?) (Henry sadly shakes head and leaves the stage with loud hiccups.) Now, to those of you who are tuning in for the first time, we want to explain how Track-an-Act works. Our trackers have been hot on the trail of talent for weeks! One by one they will present their finds to you. Listen carefully, ladies and gentlemen, for you will judge the winner by your applause.

(Usher comes forward; whistle from someone in the audience.) No whistling, please. (To the usher.) Will you please bring us our first tracker tonight? (As the usher escorts her first tracker to the platform, Henry gives another commercial.)

HENRY: Listen, ladies . . . (holds his hand to his ear). Do you hear it—that washday melody? Listen (hiccups). Then from offstage comes voices singing to the tune of "Rocked in the Cradle of the Deep."

Washed in a washer full of Bleep

My clothes are cleaned so fresh and deep—

That's enough—that's enough! What more can we say, ladies? Clothes cleaner, cleaner with Bloop-Bleep, Bleep for short. (Bows low; hiccups. Exits, muttering so the audience can hear: "Gotta do something about those hiccups.")

(During this commercial, the usher has brought the first tracker to the stage. She shakes hands with Jack and they whisper together.)

JACK: How do you do, Mrs. ————, I believe you said your name is. Well, what's in a name? A rose is a rose is a rose is a—(hiccups) Darn! Henry's hiccups must be contagious.

Pardon me, ma'am. Would you like to tell us what your hobby is? (She answers.) My hobby is my jobby! (Groan from offstage; Jack looks wounded.) Okay, okay, I can take a hint. Well, Mrs. ————, what talent have you brought us tonight?

TRACKER I: (explains her "act" who comes from front row where she is sitting. Tracker introduces her to Jack.)

JACK: Well, how do you do, Mrs. ————. Mrs., eh? You must have a husband, then. Do you know most husbands know all the answers? (Quickly) They should—they have been listening for years!

But now, tell us what you are going to do for us.

ACTOR I: (Performs and takes a seat.)

JACK: Thank you, Mrs. ————. (Sings, in a sing-song, to the same tune as the old convention favorite: "Here is table number one," etc.) Where is tracker number two, number two, number two, where is tracker number two—(Usher hurries forward with the next tracker.)

JACK: Good evening, Mrs. ————. What does your husband do for a living? (She answers) How many acres does he farm? (She answers) He must be a good provider. I asked **(local woman)** if **(her husband)** was a good provider. She said, "Sure. He's going to get some new furniture **providing** he finds a job and he's going to get a job **providing** it suits him. He's the most providing man I know!"

I guess I've been a little nosey. Let us "nose" (offstage groan) what you have for us tonight.

TRACKER 2: (Explains; introduces her contestant.)

JACK: How do you do, Mr. ————. Are you married? (The bachelor or widower performing answers) No? It's just as well. If you found a beautiful bride, she'd never look the same after she washed her face!

Welcome to our show, Mr. ————. What are you going to present for us?

ACTOR 2: (Performs and returns to his seat.)

(Usher brings forward Tracker No. 3. During this time, Henry comes on stage. He opens and closes his mouth, gestures wildly. Finally Jack holds up a placard: "Please stand by. Audio portion temporarily discontinued due to technical difficulties." Henry goes on with exaggerated gestures and opening and closing mouth. Then, as if sound has suddenly come on:

HENRY: Bloop-Bleep! (Hiccups; exits.)

JACK: Somebody needs to scare that guy. (Turns to Tracker 3 that usher introduces.) Welcome to Track-an-Act, Miss ————. Have you any family ties? (She answers) Speaking of family ties, do you know what they are? A family tie is what father buys and his son wears!

Now—what talent have you tracked down for us to enjoy?

TRACKER 3: (Explains; introduces the guest; exits.)

JACK: Welcome, welcome, young lady. How is your health? (Quickly, before she can answer.) Speaking of health, I hear **(local name)** is taking pills. He takes green pills for his stomach, purple pills for his liver, yellow pills for his feet and blue pills for his nerves. Finally he went to Doc **(local name)** who gave him some red pills to direct traffic for the rest of them!

But enough of that—tell us what pleasure we have in store.

ACTOR 3: (Performs; returns to his seat. Usher brings forward the next tracker.)

HENRY: This is Henry J. Henry again, ladies. What is that washday habit? (Loud yell: Bleep!) What gets your clothes white as a rabbit? (Loud yell: Bleep!) That's right, folks. There's nothing like it. Nothing. No, nothing beats Bloop-Bleep. (Hiccup.)

JACK: You can say that again!

HENRY: Bloop-Bleep! (Hiccups.) The Bloop that sold out to Bleep because Bleep wanted Bloop because Bleep thought that if Bloop was so good, Bleep could be a new improved Bloop! (Hiccups and exits. Tracker comes forward; the usher whispers her name to Jack.)

JACK: How do you do there, ma'am? How would you like to talk to us? (Quickly, before she can answer.) Speaking of talking, did you hear about the two women going on a plane? One of them minced her way up to the pilot (walks as if mocking her) and said to him, "Please, sir, don't go faster than sound. We want to talk."

I wonder how talkative this young fellow is. Tell the nice audience your name. Well, anyway, the audience. (Pause for the child to answer.) What subject do you like best in school? (Answer.) Know what I liked best when I was a kid? Recess!

Well, recess is over. Time to get to work. How about showing us what you can do, sonny?

ACTOR 4: (The child performs and returns to his seat.)

(As the usher brings Tracker 5 forward, Henry enters again. If you think your crowd won't object, he can carry a roll of tissue from which he pretends to read. He is almost convulsed with hiccups.)

HENRY: Laa-dies. What is the washday habit? (Hiccups.) Oh. Sorry. Lost my place. (Unrolls paper as if reading.) Here we are. (Hiccup.) Go to A. Ground Baker, the Undertaker. (Hiccup.) Oh, sorry. Wrong commercial. Wrong program. (Hiccup). Keep Bleep in the jeep to keep a heap of cheap laundry white as sheep! (Hiccups, then bows low. Someone offstage tears a piece of cloth with a loud r-rr-ip! Henry grabs the seat of his pants and rushes from the stage.)

JACK: I **told** you he needed a good scare to get rid of the hiccups! (To Tracker.) Good evening, Mrs. ————. That's a mighty pretty dress you're wearing. I'll bet it wrecked the budget! You know what a budget is—a way of going into debt systematically!

What talent have you smelled out for us? Oh, oh. That doesn't sound quite right. What talent have you tracked down?

TRACKER 5: (Explains; introduces the guest; exits.)

JACK: I have a personal question to ask you, Mr. ————. Are you married? (Man admits it.) Well, I suppose then you hardly know where your next cent is coming from. If you could account for your money, you'd be either a bookkeeper or a bachelor—certainly not a married man!

Now—how about explaining what you are going to do for us?

ACTOR 5: (Performs; leaves the stage.)

HENRY: Remember, folks, next time you go to town, call

out, "Go to town! Keep a heap of Bleep, the washday habit!" Buy it by the carton; better still, by the case. Or the truckload. Good-night, everybody. (He backs out. Jack waves and grins. Program may end here, or if you plan to sell refreshments, finish thus:)

JACK: That's about all, folks. Our sponsor tonight was Bleep, the washday habit. Our co-sponsor is (Name of organization). And now, it's time to eat! Good-night, everybody!

(Note: Winners may be judged by applause from the audience, a panel of judges or by selling votes.)

Chapter Fourteen

FASHION SHOWS

Every woman likes a fashion show! Your group has never sponsored one? So what? Just plan slowly and carefully, and work out all the details.

Your first step, as with all projects, is to plan and appoint committees. If you're featuring hand-sewn garments (after a class, for example), obtaining them is no problem. Otherwise, you'll need a committee in charge of getting the clothes. The committee can contact local stores. You can usually find at least one store that is eager to co-operate for the publicity.

Be sure to get in touch with an executive. Possibilities are the buyer, store manager, promotion manager, advertising manager, or a director of women's activities. Of course, you'll have your plans well worked out first. To help sell the store's representative on your idea, tell him the expected attendance, tentative date, size of the room, etc. He will also want to know about how many models you'll use. Explain how you plan to publicize the show. Emphasize that the store will be given credit in publicity and during the program.

Make appointments for models to be fitted and designate the exact type garments needed. Arrange for suitable accessories while you're at it. The models will need hats, gloves, bags, and jewelry. You may have to contact other stores, too. Re-assure all who help that they will be given proper credit.

You'll need a large room for the show. Consider the school auditorium, a local hotel, public hall, civic center, or theater. Perhaps the co-operating store has its own auditorium.

Arrange for proper lighting, a spotlight for models, and curtains. In an auditorium, you'll want a microphone and a reading stand for the commentator. They might not be essential in a smaller room but check to be sure everything can be heard.

Script

Almost as important as smart fashions and lovely models is a good script. Lucky is the club that has a talented writer.

The script should call attention to various details of design, construction, the fabric, colors, sizes available, and perhaps the cost. You might even mention care of the fabric.

All facts must be woven into a clever, chatty style. Usually from 50 to 85 words is enough description for each garment. Mention each model's name unless you have printed programs with the information.

Of course it is impossible to give a fashion show script here. It depends on the clothing you use, your facilities, and other factors. You'll probably find it is easier to write an interesting script if you plan the show around a theme. (More about that later.)

The store might furnish the commentator. If not, choose one of your own members who reads well. It is even better if she can memorize enough that she doesn't have to read, word for word. The commentator should have a clear, strong voice and pleasing personality. If you wish, she may be hidden be-hind the stage. This is sometimes better, especially if an "outsider" would detract from the story being acted by the models. If the script has no particular story, the commentator might chat about the clothes in her own words. This is a friendly, informal way to handle it.

Try for special features you can work in for added interest. Twins are a natural, if available. A family of stairstep-sized girls also makes a good feature, or a three-generation group. A wedding is a nice climax to a fashion show but it has been used a lot.

Models

Select your models carefully. If possible, have a model for each garment to eliminate changing. However, it is more important to have a few pretty, poised girls than many inadequate models. If they must double up, be sure their appearances are spaced to allow time to change.

You'll probably need at least five models. They may be from your club or from a local school. Perhaps you can tie in with a clothing class. Choose girls or women who can wear standard sizes without alteration. They should have poise, and enjoy modeling.

The directing may be done by a high school dramatics teacher or other expert. Don't frighten amateurs with a lot of professional advice. They're liable to act stiff and unnatural. Just teach them one thing—correct posture. Head should be up, chest out, hips and stomach in. Hands should hang loosely at the sides when not busy.

If the models concentrate on standing straight and tall, with tummy in, they'll do okay. They might get a kick out of walking with a book on their heads to develop a "glide." Show the girls the proper posture, then let them practice before the other models.

Decide with the script writers how models should enter and exit. Two might come in together but focus attention on only one at a time.

Remember, the audience wants back views, too. Models should turn around on the stage any way that seems natural. Rest one foot at a slight angle from the other when standing still.

The girls should look as if they're enjoying themselves. A forced smile is better than none. Just hope the audience is far enough away to think the smile is genuine!

The young women should wear make-up. They'll need more than usual if the show is at night under artificial light. Insist on chic, attractive hairstyles. Naturally they'll avoid underarm hair with sleeveless styles, leg hair with bathing suits or shorts.

Work out a path. You will probably want the models to go to the center of the stage, pause, walk to one side and turn. Then they should walk to the opposite side and turn. If the room has only a central aisle, have models stop once near the front, then about midway or beyond for their turns. Warn them not to walk or turn too fast.

Timing is important because the models should follow the script. Several tricks for showing special features are: hold out full skirts with one hand—palms away from the audience—to do a turn; casually point to any special detail mentioned; insert hand, with thumb showing, in a pocket.

Of course you'll see to suitable accessories. Street costumes should have hats and gloves, sports outfits usually don't. And if a model has to remove a coat to show the dress underneath, it will be awkward for her to handle a purse.

Dream up things to be carried such as traveling bags, tennis racket, picnic basket, mixing bowl, etc. These props give the models something to do with their hands and add interest.

Line up exactly what the girls will need. They may wear their own shoes but they must be appropriate. The models might also wear their own jewelry, if it's suitable. Each girl should have a list of her needs.

Plan ample space for changing clothes. Set up card tables for accessories and props, racks for garments. Provide a full-view mirror, as well as smaller mirrors and good light for making up.

Assistants

You'll need backstage assistants. The store may send a representative to be sure the models get clothes on exactly right. The assistants should have a list of all garments and models in order of their appearance. They'll also want a list of accessories that goes with each costume.

The assistants make sure garments are pressed and ready to go. They also help the girls get into their clothes. They check supplies of hangers, dress shields, and cleansing tissues.

One assistant should have a marked copy of the script to give models their cues. The other assistant gives a final check. Make sure hair is in place, stocking seams straight, and everything under control.

Of course you'll caution models and assistants to be careful of garments. (Watch out for lipstick or perspiration stains.) The store was generous enough to co-operate so return their goods in the best condition. Appoint someone to pack the garments after the show, unless the store does it.

Background

Music is important. It makes modeling easier to move in rhythm. Music also adds atmosphere or helps carry out your theme. A member might play the piano. Or you could use a phonograph; it must be watched constantly. Another possibility is a high school, college, or local orchestra.

All music should be in slow, walking time. Keep it soft so the commentator can be heard easily.

It's a good idea to have a musical advisor on the script-writing committee. They can tie theme songs in with the script to carry out the story or describe the garments. For example, a brunch coat might call for "Oh, What a Beautiful Morning," and a smart raincoat, "Singing in the Rain." It's best to use a well-known song if the lyrics are to describe clothing or story.

If you want the music simply as background and atmosphere, any soft selections are appropriate.

Be sure to have at least one rehearsal. Everyone needs to know her cues and exact duties. Models need not wear the garments, but they should practice walking, entrances, and exits. The commentator should read the script, too.

Publicity

One good means of publicity is the ticket-selling. Put all members to work! Distribute posters in the post office, stores, and other buildings. Provide both advance and follow-up notices to newspapers, radio and TV stations. Furnish society or fashion editors with free tickets. Suggest they take photographs for the paper.

And for goodness sakes, don't forget to credit the store who is working with you!

If you expect an audience of several hundred, assign ushers. Members of your club will probably be glad to serve. Teen-age girls usually like to dress up in formal gowns as ushers.

If you decide on printed programs, list the type of garment (in the order it is shown), along with the name of the model. You might even give a descriptive word or two. For example:

1. Shocking pink Bermuda shorts modeled by Betty Smith.
2. Turquoise Dacron street dress modeled by Ruth Adams.

At the bottom of the program, give credit to the co-operating store.

If you feel your show is too small to warrant programs, the commentator can give credit to the store and models.

Even a small group can have a satisfactory fashion show. Hold an informal discussion after the modeling. The audience can then ask questions of the commentator or store representative. If you like, follow the discussion period with a tea.

Themes for Fashion Shows

As mentioned before, a theme helps keep a fashion show moving. No doubt you can think of several ideas, but we list some for you.

Mother-Daughter Style Show

Pair mothers and daughters off to model the clothes, or use them as commentators. You might even use a mother-daughter musical combination (such as soloist and accompanist). This fashion show is particularly appropriate near Mother's Day.

Family Album

A grandmother behind a "frame" looks at her ancestors in their new clothes. She can be in the background throughout, and perhaps even be a "talking ghost" commenting after each model exits.

Time

This is always a natural. Consider a "Fashions 'Round the Clock," "A Week of Styles," or just about time in general. You can call it "The Time of Your Life." Build a huge clock for background, about eight feet tall. Arrange steps in front of it, potted palms on either side. Heavy draperies can form an effective background. The models walk up the steps and down again.

Brides of Yesterday

At this show, the garments come out of the attic! Daughters or young friends can model any dresses that owners have outgrown. You could even send make-believe wedding invitations

to the show. The commentators or wearer tells the owner's love story. Or give this information about each gown: name of owner, name of model, year gown was worn. Tell interesting facts about the dress, the wedding, or the year it took place. Women will also be interested in the fabric, and who made the dress. Music can suggest the year the gown was first worn. Of course you'll use traditional wedding music.

It would be appropriate to have a tea table decorated with a wedding cake. Serve with it hot tea, coffee or punch, depending on the weather. Arrange chairs as pews and let the "brides" actually march down the aisle.

Pay special recognition to the newest and oldest brides present. Ask members to bring clippings of their wedding write-ups for display.

TV Shows

Many television shows would make a good theme. You might conduct "This Is Your Life," with the models coming out of the subject's past. There are many quiz shows you can work out. Or arrange the background for any fashion show as a television studio. Then let the "cameras" roll!

Watch the Birdie

A photographer's studio makes a good setting. Each model supposedly comes in to pose for a photo—a good excuse for dressing up! The commentator can act as the photographer. Or you can have another person take the part, pantomiming without speaking.

Topper's Parade

Only hats are featured. Models wear plain, dark dresses so emphasis is on the hats. The models could appear in a picture frame arrangement to show heads only. For amusement, show some funny old-fashioned hats along with the modern ones. A millinery department of a store might sponsor this show.

All Ages

Children can get into the act at fashion shows. Pretending to play "drop the handkerchief" is a wonderful way to show backs of dresses. Older models can pass along a tea table, supposedly set up on the same lawn.

Tea for You

Card tables were set up around the room at this fashion show. Guests went to the tea table for cookies and beverage. They took them to the smaller tables where they sat and watched the show.

Each table was decorated with a miniature May pole centerpiece. There was soft, appropriate music throughout the affair. The stage represented a yard with a beach umbrella and lawn chairs. Two ladies stood in the yard and chatted with each model as she came in. The conversation, of course, was about the garments. No commentator was used. Models displayed the clothes by walking on across the stage, then down among the tables where they sat with the audience.

Hobbies

Let each model illustrate a different hobby. For example, a girl in skirt and overblouse could be painting at an easel.

Sugar-Coated Show

The models illustrate good manners as they show off the clothes. For example, the commentator explains how to make introductions as the models act it out. This theme is good for a youthful audience.

Chapter Fifteen

FOOD AS A MONEY-MAKER

Every time women get together to raise money, food usually enters into the plans. The Girl Scouts sell cookies and the club has bake sales. Many churches get more profit from the bazaar supper than from the sale of handiwork. One of the most popular "food sales" is serving the community meal. It is served for schools, clubs, churches, lodges. The list is practically endless, as you know.

Delicious, profitable quantity meals don't just happen. There's never been a Topsy "just-growed" one yet! A profitable big meal must be planned right down to the last detail.

What is a truly successful community dinner made of? Capable chairmen and hard-working women! You also need enthusiasm, organization, wise buying, good cooking, satisfied guests, and a reasonable profit.

Choose as general chairman a capable woman that is a natural-born leader. It helps if she has a knack for good food and attractive service. She should be enthusiastic about the project, well acquainted with people, and have time to handle the job. It would be foolish to put in charge a mother of many small children.

The general chairman should use the following rule: Plan **what** is to be done, by **whom** it is to be done, and **where** it is to be done.

She should divide work and responsibility by appointing committees, then co-ordinate their work. That means she supervises and doesn't exhaust herself trying to do it all.

It's a good idea to make a written work schedule for each committee chairman. Make a report of the dinner after it is over, too. Include the financial report and any suggestions learned the hard way.

The general chairman appoints committees. This list is merely a suggestion. You may find a division of duties that works better in your case. For example, you may prefer having the planning committee plan the menu, too. And maybe it will work out better for you to have the publicity committee sell tickets.

At least you'll need someone responsible for all these duties, no matter how they're divided:

Planning and arrangements; publicity; kitchen committee (menu planning and preparation); dining room (table settings, waitresses); clean-up; finance and tickets.

Planning and Arrangements Committee

Begin making plans a month in advance, if possible. This committee can send out invitations, if used. Send cards to your own membership, if you wish. Personal invitation by telephone is always good. You'll need a telephone committee. Of course if the meal you are serving is for another organization, they'll take care of promoting attendance.

The place? Community hall, school lunchroom or gym, lodge hall, church basement. Is there a kitchen with adequate equipment? If not, don't give up. Perhaps you can arrange to have women cook the food in their own kitchens. Sometimes you can make arrangements with a local cafe or baker to do part of the work.

Decide on a date (unless a group is hiring you to serve for a specific occasion) and set a deadline for reservations. Even though approximate, these are most important for a successful affair.

Publicity Committee

See chapter on publicity.

Kitchen Committee

This committee is responsible for menu planning, marketing, and food preparation.

Choose the menu carefully. Keep in mind the type of affair, cost, equipment and space available, and number of people who will be working. Try for food that can mostly be prepared ahead of time. Choose food that won't spoil if there is a delay. Serve contrasts such as hot and cold, tart and sweet, fat and acid. You'll want good flavor combinations. And don't use colors that clash on the plate.

Simple garnishes add a party touch. Hot rolls help to glamorize a plain meal, as does a fancy dessert. If you have menus that have been popular and profitable, keep them on file.

Here are some things to avoid in planning your community meal menu: molded desserts or salads (unless you can keep them chilled until the minute they're served); meringue-topped pies; dressing-drowned, wilted salads (keep ingredients crisp and cold, adding dressing at last minute). Don't serve unusual foods that many people may not like, elaborate foods that are difficult to fix and serve, hard-to-digest foods. Avoid heavy foods for all-women groups, too-light meals for men.

Don't serve creamed foods and cream pies in extremely hot weather, as there is chance of food poisoning. Never let food stand very long at room temperature. Refrigeration is a must.

Keep all perishables there until the last minute before serving.

Choose approved, tested recipes for quantity. Don't simply multiply a family recipe for five by ten to serve 50. You'll need a recipe especially worked out for 50 people. Many companies furnish such recipes.

Marketing

Compile a detailed market list. Divide into foods to be purchased and to be donated. For economy, buy in as large quantity as possible. Ask your grocer to help you; he may quote wholesale prices. Get figures before buying. The finance committee will want to know approximate cost of food to decide on the price to charge.

Non-perishable foods can be delivered the day beforehand. Better have a "checker." He should provide a central place for storing and should check bills and items against the marketing list. In case of error, notify the store immediately. This gives time to re-order so food can still be delivered in time. Use a checking system for donated foods, too. Be sure owner's name is on any containers she wants returned.

Make sure you can return unused packaged and canned goods. You may have to pay a deposit on bottles so don't forget to return them. Pay all bills as promptly as possible.

Cooking

Of course your committee is composed of good cooks who don't panic in an emergency or when rushed. They should wear comfortable shoes and clothing. It's understood they'll have on clean wash dresses and aprons. Food handlers are also supposed to wear hair nets. Insist on constant hand-washing and all sanitary measures. Use paper towels instead of a common hand towel. If a worker turns up with a cold or skin infection, send her home!

Cooking. Food handlers wear clean, comfortable clothing and shoes, and hair nets.

Ask workers to limit conversation during the busiest time. There is nothing worse than a bunch of "yakety" women getting in each other's way. Later, as they eat, they can chat to their hearts' content.

Have a Super Chef, or whatever you wish to call her. She should oversee and organize. It might even be helpful to have a list posted of exact time each food is to go into the oven. Arrange, somehow, for the food to reach the table HOT. The biggest criticism of many quantity meals is lukewarm food that should be hot.

Taste all foods before serving. You may cook by guess and by gosh at home, but here everything must be exact. Insist on level measurements. In quantities, weighing sometimes is quicker than measuring.

If you have to dole out cooking among the members to do in their own kitchens, ask all to use the same recipe. This makes for uniformity. And of course you'll make sure the best cooks in your group get the job! A food failure or two can ruin your reputation as a serving group in a hurry.

You may want to sub-divide the cooks as follows: meat cook, cooks meat and any accompanying gravy or dressing. Vegetable cook, prepares and cooks vegetables. Salad chef, prepares all ingredients, dressing, and relishes. Then she tosses or garnishes the salad just before serving. (It's a good idea to keep cut, fresh vegetables crisp under a damp cloth sprinkled with ice.) Bread and butter lady makes or heats purchased rolls; or slices bread. (To keep rolls warm in oven without drying out, cover with a damp towel.) She also makes sure there is butter, salt, and pepper for every table.

Beverage-maker prepares the coffee and makes sure each table has sugar and cream. It is up to her to watch the supply and be ready to make more if needed.

Dessert supervisor. If pies or cakes are donated, insist on the best. If not donated, this woman prepares or buys the dessert. Ice cream can be purchased and is a favorite dessert. She should get a good ice cream dip before she gets ready to serve it! Extra tip: use wet scissors to cut sticky foods such as marshmallows or raisins.

Dishing Up

This requires a definite system. Each cook should know exactly what she is to do. Here again a posted list helps. A good sequence for arranging foods on the stove, steam table or serving table is as follows: stack of plates, meat, potatoes, vegetables, gravy, beverage. Salads and rolls are usually placed on the dining tables, rather than on the plates. This method is for the waitress-type service where the plates are filled in the kitchen and carried to the dining room.

For family service, fill serving bowls for each table. Guests pass the food, helping themselves. You'll still need a few waitresses to fill water glasses, pour coffee, replenish supplies.

If you use the third type service—cafeteria or buffet— arrange foods on a table from which guests are served. Or they can help themselves. A convenient line-up is trays, silver wrapped in napkin, water, meat, potatoes, vegetables, bread, butter, dessert, beverage. Guests carry their trays to the tables. Have a few waitresses to carry trays of youngsters and the elderly, and to refill beverages, etc.

Regardless of which serving method you use, you **must** be organized to keep things moving smoothly and people out of each other's way.

If you serve more than 75 guests, you may need a "double setup." This can be both sides of one table, or two tables.

It helps keep food hot to warm plates beforehand. Use ladels, large serving spoons, or ice cream scoops so servings will be uniform size.

Serve plates as fast as waitresses, or guests, can pick them up. One or more persons should be appointed to replenish food as the servers run out.

Dining Room

This committee might secure tables, chairs, linens, dishes and silver. They should oversee the waitresses and set tables. These same women can be the table decorations committee, and hostess committee, or that might be assigned elsewhere.

In setting up the dining room, be sure to leave enough room between tables for waitresses. Four feet between tables allows about 18 inches for passing between backs of chairs when guests are seated. You can leave even more space for a main aisle or two, if you wish.

Make a list several weeks in advance of tablecloths, dishes, silver, and glassware needed. If your club or the kitchen you'll be using doesn't provide enough, then begin your campaign to borrow. BE SURE to identify all property. Take the best of care of all borrowed items and return them promptly. If you need special punch bowls or elaborate service, check a rental service.

If the people you're serving aren't your own, they may provide their own hostesses. If not, they'll appreciate this committee taking wraps, greeting the guests, and helping to seat them. Better check.

If this committee is to see to centerpieces, remember the most beautiful thing on any table is flowers. If they're out of season, consider buying. Perhaps a local florist will give you a special rate. If the dinner is a banquet, chances are the group having it will provide decorations on a specific theme.

In setting the tables, remember to allow 20 to 24 inches of table space per person.

Even though dishes don't match, be sure they're sparkly clean and free from cracks. Use matching dishes for each place setting, if possible, and you'll be surprised how uniform it looks. If you have enough of a kind to alternate the settings, that's even better. Or perhaps you can handle one whole table with one pattern of dishes, another table with another.

Waitresses

Some groups provide their own waitresses (such as at a Junior-Senior banquet when underclassmen often serve). At any rate, the dining room committee should supervise the waitresses. Ask them to come early and give them complete instructions beforehand.

Insist on quiet, fast service. Draw a chart showing the assignment of waitresses to tables. One waitress can usually serve from 10 to 12 guests. Before the guests are seated, each waitress should check the table setting and pour water. Two to three ice cubes to a glass keep water cold, even though poured early. Waitresses place butter, jelly, salads, sugar and cream. A teapot or small coffee pot is handy to pour cream into the small cream pitchers. If the first course is cold, it should be on the table when guests sit down. If a hot soup, naturally it is served after they are seated.

Do organize a service line in the kitchen for the waitresses. Arrange a dining room "step-saver"—a small cart or table with water for refilling glasses, coffee pots (on a burner to keep it hot, if possible), etc.

It might be convenient to serve through a service window, or across a Dutch door, to keep waitresses out of the kitchen. You can even put a table across the door between the kitchen and dining room. Waitresses pick up food from this table.

They carry main course plates to the dining room on trays or two at a time in the hands. Direct waitresses to follow each other and place a plate next to where the last one left off. They move right until all are served. Other waitresses should follow with rolls and coffee or other beverage. Waitresses return to their assigned spots to serve refills of beverages and rolls.

General rules for waitresses:

1. Serve and remove all foods with the left hand, from left side of guest.

2. Serve and remove all beverages with the right hand, from right side. Refill water glasses without removing from table.

3. Try to anticipate needs of the guests assigned to you.

4. Handle dishes and silverware as quietly as possible.

5. Remove all dishes and silver from one place setting at a time. Use left hand, from left side of guests. Do not stack dishes in front of him. Stack like-dishes together, heaviest in the center on the tray, and carry to the dishwashers. (One waitress might hold the tray while another picks up the dishes and places them on it.) A small truck or cart on wheels is a great energy saver in transporting heavy loads.

6. Pick up cups by the handles and glasses at the base. Keep fingers and thumbs off the inside of plates and bowls.

7. Personal neatness and cleanliness is a must.

8. Avoid unnecessary talking while serving.

9. If there is a program, BE QUIET.

If the waitresses aren't interested in the program, dismiss them after they carry the last loads of dirty dishes to the kitchen.

Clean-up Committee

This committee is self-explanatory! Change members from time to time as naturally it's the least fun. But it is important. You want to leave the kitchen—whether church, school or club-room kitchen—as good or better than you found it.

The clean-up committee takes over after all are served. Don't wait until the evening is over to start! Pots and pans can be washed, garbage emptied, etc., before serving dishes are brought to the kitchen. Dishwashing goes faster in a tidy kitchen.

Make sure there is enough space for dirty dishes as they're brought from the dining room. You'll need a scraper, garbage container, facilities for proper dishwashing, and PLENTY of hot water. Use a good quality soap or synthetic detergent.

Scrape and stack dishes as they're brought from the dining room. Rinse the dishes before washing to keep dishwasher clean and to loosen food particles. It makes washing easier. Soak silver in a pan of warm soapy water; it will be a snap to wash.

Wash dishes in this order: glassware, silverware, small dishes, large dishes, utensils (unless already done).

Water should be hot as the hands can stand. Change the water often, as it cools and becomes greasy. Scald dishes in hot water (170° to 180° F.). Of course this is hotter than your hand can take. Stack dishes in a wire tray or container with handles; dip the tray into the pan or sink. Use a thermometer to be sure of temperature. This process sterilizes the dishes. Check local and state laws to see if a special chemical rinse is required for sterilization. If not, the hot water treatment will do.

Authorities say it is best to let dishes dry by themselves. If your accommodations don't permit this method, use lots of dry, clean towels. Boil or wash immediately after using.

You should probably divide the crew as follows: one person to scrape dishes, one to rinse and stack, one to load dishes and wash in machine (or at least two if washing by hand), one to each dishwasher to dry and stack. Assign one to put dishes away or divide for returning to owners.

Finance

This committee may sell the tickets. It's a good idea to sell most of them in advance. There is liable to be confusion and delay over collecting money at the door. However, plan to sell a few at the time, too.

To determine how much you should charge, get the marketing list and approximate costs from the kitchen committee.

Here's one method for setting your price. Add cost of food, napkins, decorations, fuel, laundry, and other incidental charges. If some food is donated, it should be included in the cost. Now, double the total amount. Divide by the number of people you expect. (It seldom pays to serve less than 25.) This price should give plenty of margin for expenses and profit.

If members donate their services for all the work involved, your group should clear about 50% of the receipts. If you do, you know you've put on a successful community meal!

Perhaps there is a customary charge in your community of say a dollar per plate. If you figure you can't keep food costs to about 40% of gross receipts at a dollar per, then start hunting another menu!

Avoid giving away too many free meals.

Avoid giving away too many free meals. Have your policy clearly understood. Should all workers eat for free? Perhaps, but certainly not their families. (You might offer a special feature of children's plates at half price.) Whatever you decide, stick with it.

Food for Fifty

	Each Serving	For 50
Butter	1/3 oz. serving	1½ lbs.
Coffee	1 cup per person	1½ lbs., 2½ gals. water
Cream for coffee	2 tablespoons	1½ qts. cream, ½ cup milk
Cream, whipping	2 tablespoons	1 qt.
Beef, veal, pork (for roasting)	4 to 5 oz.	20 lbs.
Bread		3 loaves
Ice cream, bulk		2 gals.
Ground meat		15 lbs.
Hot, ham		20 lbs.
Olives, pickles		½ gal.
Potato chips		3½ lbs.
Potato salad		9 qts.
Salad dressing		1 qt.
Sugar		1 lb.
Tea		¼ lb.
Vegetables, canned		10 qts., 3 #10 cans
Cabbage for slaw		16 lbs.
Roast turkey or chicken		30 lbs., drawn wt.
Tomatoes for salad		10 lbs.
Lettuce under salad (1 leaf)		4 to 5 heads

Other Food Fund-Raisers

There are other means of selling food besides community meals, of course.

Bake Sale

Have contributors label cake as Chocolate with Lemon Icing, or whatever. People like to know what they're buying. One group had the women attach a card with the recipe! Write the donor's name on a piece of adhesive tape. Stick it on the bottom of the cake plate, so she'll be sure to have it returned to her.

Price? One group solved the problem by having three price ranges. Highest price was for the biggest, most attractive cakes; moderate price for average size and appearance; lowest to small cakes or those damaged en route.

Have plenty of clean cardboard boxes and paper bags. Don't put all cakes and pies out at once. Otherwise those who come first will have the biggest selection, and latecomers will find only those left over.

Don't "put aside" certain foods for friends. If you insist, don't leave the sold food out in open sight. It's annoying to want to buy something only to find it is already sold or promised.

However, if a cake is beautifully decorated you may want to keep it on display. If the buyer is in no hurry to take it, mark it plainly "Sold."

Don't sell a bakery cake as homemade. The public resents being fooled.

If necessary, cut a cake and sell half. Charge slightly more than half price for each half.

Bargain Basement Supper

Instead of the usual community meal to make money, sell a 9-cent sale meal. Serve cafeteria style with prices plainly

A bargain basement supper is bound to appeal to one and all—especially the thrifty.

marked. Items of food you would expect to see for 10 cents, label 9 cents, 50 cents—49. In other words, keep all prices uneven numbers to seem like a bigger bargain!

Chicken and Noodles

One club is noted for its delicious chicken and homemade noodles. The townspeople look forward to the event that takes place about twice a year. With this, the ladies serve a simple salad, dessert, and coffee.

A Hot Dog Wagon

This feature really made money for one group. Members take turns running it. They "park" it near a factory, and the employes flock to it.

Cook Some Cash!

Bake and deliver birthday cakes on order. Members take turns baking them. Have a chairman who takes orders, and then phones the request to the member whose turn it is. If baking is inconvenient for her at that time, she can trade her "turn" with another member.

Ice Cream Social

This one is so obvious it seems hardly necessary to mention it. It is usually held on the church lawn, school yard, an empty lot, or roped-off section of the street. If weather does not permit, any public building does the job. The usual menu is homemade ice cream, cakes, pie, and coffee. This is a natural money-maker when there are rural club women who have plenty of milk and cream for the ice cream. Usually the women, and even their little girls, get a kick out of being "waitresses." But don't forget to appoint dishwashers—they're necessary, too. The greatest precautions should be taken to keep food and dishes clean and sanitary.

Catering

One group supplied fancy sandwiches and delicacies to businesswomen for their special luncheons or meetings. The club charged a fairly high price for this catering service. They bought most of the food rather than asking for donations. They felt the extra work of preparing fancy dishes was enough to ask members to contribute!

Tradition in Foods

If your community is noted for a particular food, take advantage of it. Perhaps you can start a feast that will become an annual affair. For example, in Wisconsin Norwegian communities the "ludefisk" and "lefse" suppers draw hundreds of people. Chicken fries are well known in southern Illinois and Colorado Springs has its famous chuck wagon suppers in the Garden of the Gods.

Election Doughnuts

One organization fries doughnuts right in the large community hall where the election is held. Voters can either buy a doughnut and coffee on the spot, or a sack of doughnuts to take with them.

Profit-Hunting

Many societies serve food at public farm sales and auctions. One group was waiting with hot food when hunters came in from a fox hunt. Needless to say the soup, coffee and pie sold in a flash! Hunting and cold air are bound to bring big appetites.

Roadside Market

If you live in a state such as Vermont, specialize in maple syrup for tourists. Of course you can include fruits and vegetables, but feature your community's specialty. When you set up a roadside stand, remember you must have plenty of parking space. Stands should be attractive and well-kept.

Signs are all-important to attract attention. It probably would be a good idea to have one done professionally. Uneven, dim letters give the whole project an amateur effect. The sign can be as near as 150 feet. You may want several farther away, indicating there is a roadside stand ahead.

Set up a definite schedule and make it stick. Surveys show that heaviest traffic is from 3 p.m. to 8 p.m. Of course on weekends and holidays, cars go by in a fairly steady stream.

It's a good idea for customers to order ahead, especially on baked goods. Have a variety of prices. Go a little easy with gourmet, expensive delicacies. Include some budget foods. Everything should be plainly labeled with weight and price.

You'll need to protect products from flies and dust. If you sell perishable foods, refrigeration is essential.

Popular roadside items are dressed poultry, butter, cream, cottage cheese. Also popular are canned fruits and vegetables, herbs, jellies, jams and cider. Baked goods that sell are breads. cakes, cookies, pies and pastries.

Lunch-Packin' Mammas

Members of one club realize working women get tired of "eating out." They love homemade food. Every two weeks the club women prepare lunches to order. These are delivered, since most of the customers work within a few blocks of each other. Members take turns serving on this lunch-packing committee.

Catering Possibilities:

Box lunches for office or factory workers.

Home-cooked lunches for office workers (on telephone order).

Casserole dinners for "moving day."

Picnic baskets.

School lunches packed daily.

Hot dinners delivered to bachelors.

Boxes to send to students.

Wedding or any special-occasion cakes.

Angel food cake.

Cookies like grandma made.

Special holiday fruit cakes and plum puddings.

Serving a meal-in-a-dish.

Sunday brunches.

Saturday night suppers for college students.

Setting tea tables for women's groups.

Once-a-week dinner for employed girls.

Old-fashioned taffy pulls for teen-agers.

Delivering hot drinks and soups to fall picnics.

Chapter Sixteen

COOKBOOKS

A cookbook gives you the best recipes in town! Women in the church or community offer their prize recipes for a club cookbook. It's usually a best-seller in any community. You know how often you label your recipes, "Aunt Jane's good pudding," or "Mrs. Smith's spicy cake." In the same way, donors' names add to the appeal of the club cookbook.

A Cookbook gives you the best recipes in town! It's a big job to print a cookbook, but it probably will be the best seller locally of the year. Women love to share recipes and to see their names in print.

It's a big job, printing a cookbook. So don't even consider it unless you have lots of hard-working members. You'll also need the services of a helpful, friendly printer.

Style

Decide if your workers, and finances, allow you to have an elaborate cookbook. If your book is to be large, don't limit the recipes to members. Let them ask their relatives, friends, and people who have moved away.

Cookbooks don't have to be large or fancy if you have a small group. Small booklets and folders can be done by an inexpensive process. Mimeograph is a little difficult to read, and almost illegible when on both sides of the paper. Offset and multilith are easily read, attractive, and not as expensive as regular printing.

A booklet is good for recipes on a single subject. You might do a new booklet every year or so. First, try "Jiffy Meals." Let each member contribute her favorite quick recipe. The next time, you could do "Puddin' N' Pie," the next "Cake Talk." Remember, catchy titles help sell a book.

Format

Remember a book that opens to lie flat is handy. Ask your printer about bindings that allow it. You may also want a waterproof, washable cover. Perhaps members can make them of plastic material.

Timing

Don't even think of putting out a cookbook in much less than a year. In addition to gathering recipes, there are hours of proofreading, checking, etc., involved.

Committees

Each committee should have a definite job. The committees will depend on the size of your book and other factors. Here are suggestions:

1. General chairman. She makes arrangements with printer and co-ordinates all committees.

2. Finances. Committee members set the price, after the printer has given the chairman his estimate. Allow for a little profit but try to keep the book cheap enough to encourage sáles.

(If your club is too small for a separate sales committee, the finance committee can be in charge of sales when the books are printed.)

3. Advertising and promotion. Advertising by local merchants, and even those of neighboring towns, will help considerably on profit. Make the decision of how much to charge per page. Assign territories to your "advertising salesmen." Alternate pages of recipes and ads.

Sometimes small ads across the bottom of a page are easier to sell them big ads. Although bringing in less, enough of them do count up. Chances are your printer may help you estimate a price to charge for advertising.

The committee should make a "dummy" cookbook, exactly the planned size, with squares outlined for the ads. Penciled horizontal lines indicate the recipes. And don't forget an index or table of contents.

If you decide to publish one of the smaller booklets mentioned, you may not need any advertising to finance it.

4. Recipe collecting. Members should co-operate by giving their favorite recipes. Here's how one group handled it: each club member sent three of her favorite recipes to the committee, who selected one from each.

Be sure to have several superior cooks on this committee. They'll be able to weed out incorrect recipes. Make it a **must** that all recipes must be tested and found successful. You'll only be doing your club harm to print recipes that "won't work."

Allow this committee a long time to choose from the many

recipes. Chances are the recipes will sort of fall into categories as you begin to sort them.

5. Editorial and proofreading. This committee works with the printer. If you have someone in your group with journalism experience, so much the better. She can write an introduction, and possibly other text besides recipes. Have the recipes edited and typed, all in the same style. For example, if you list ingredients first, then the directions, do it throughout the book. Abbreviations should be consistent, too. (If one recipe has one tbsp. for tablespoon, all recipes should.)

Proofreading is merely reading the printed papers or "proofs" the printer gives you. Don't make last-minute minor changes—only real corrections. Some printers charge extra for changes. But of course you do not want any errors. Two people should read proofs together. One holds the proof she is checking, the other the original recipe. Read aloud—word for word, cup for cup—each and every recipe. Also check spelling of women's names. When you are positive there are no mistakes, return the proof so the printer can go ahead.

Incidentally, if you're wondering how to mark a mistake, you'll find proofreader's marks in the back of most dictionaries.

6. Sales committee. When the cookbook is finished, announce it with fanfare! You might feature the cookbook at a food sale, selling dishes prepared from recipes printed in the book. Perhaps a radio or TV station can help promote it. You may find a local book store willing to sell it, displaying it in their window. Suggest them as gifts.

Be sure to have plenty of copies of your cookbook at all functions your sponsor. Set up a cookbook booth at your carnival or bazaar, a table of them at your home talent play. The sales committee will carry on, but each member should consider herself a committee of one to sell the cookbook.

Chapter Seventeen

PUBLICITY FOR PAYING PROJECTS

The publicity committee is most important for any money-making event. The success of the project depends on getting it before the public. Many times women contribute a lot of time and work. Then they buy back their own bazaar contributions simply because not enough outsiders attended. No matter how much effort goes into an event, if nobody knows, nobody comes!

Remember in any publicity, the word YOU is important. People are inclined to wonder, "What's in it for me?" Are you offering fun? Education? Prizes?

The work of the committee begins as soon as the plans are made. If you're doing a large affair, you'll need an entire publicity committee. If a smaller project, perhaps the publicity chairman can handle it alone.

Don't put "all your eggs in one basket." You shouldn't rely on only one form of publicity and advertising. There are many mediums, of course. No doubt you are familiar with most of them.

Newspapers

The first thought, when it comes to promoting 'most anything, is the local newspapers.

Advertising

Whenever your club puts on shows for which admission is charged, the newspaper may consider the story as "advertising." Prices should never be mentioned in a news story. So it's a good idea to include some paid ads along with the free publicity you want. You'll probably get more co-operation.

Consider small "locals" scattered in with the reading material. These several-line items are read right along with the news. If yours is a big daily, there may be a section for such items.

Large display ads are attention-getters, but you probably can't consider them unless you have a fairly large budget. If you can afford such advertising, follow the advice of the newspaper's ad man. He probably knows more about copy and layout than you do!

Types of News Items

Publicity is certainly more effective before than after! But if the event was a huge success, a follow-up story is good promotion for the future. When you plan your next project, readers will remember the name of your club.

Someone may think, "The BMC Club? Oh, yes. They're the bunch who sponsored that crazy fair that was so much fun!"

As soon as you're appointed publicity chairman, check with the editor. If it's a small town paper, he'll probably know you. If not, or if a large daily, go in and introduce yourself. Ask for suggestions. He'll probably be glad to give you a few minutes to explain his pet peeves.

Most large dailies have jobs specialized. No doubt you'll be referred to the society editor, or even a club editor, when you state your business.

For follow-up stories of big projects, newspapers send their own reporters. To be sure they do, give the society editor free tickets! It helps to seat a press representative next to a loyal member who can help fill in the details. Give the editor a program or any available material concerning the event. Be sure your affair is large enough or unusual enough to be newsworthy.

And of course that is the first question the "press agent" should ask: What does the newspaper print? News, of course. If there's a real story, the paper will use it.

Someone on the committee should have a "nose for news," realize what is newsworthy. She also should know how to get the co-operation of the editors in getting the story printed.

Perhaps if your committee members aren't experienced on news reporting, you can find a young reporter (on a large paper) to help.

The first item you give the papers should tell about the plans, including appointment of committees.

Preparing Copy

Ask the paper's deadline—and observe it! Large affairs can be publicized for several weeks beforehand, shorter announcements a few days before the event.

Copy in written form promotes accuracy. Names and dates can get twisted over the telephone. (Then, too, you may find the editor's telephone is usually busy!) Spell out any name or word that might be misunderstood. Some letters are especially hard to tell apart. Examples: M and N; P and T; V, B and D; F and S. Identify letters by saying something like "P as in paper."

Do try to get publicity down on paper whenever possible. Here are a few general rules in writing copy:

1. Use a typewriter if you have one. If not, perhaps you can borrow. Hand-written copy is hard for editors and typesetters to read. It often makes for errors.

If you must hand-write lines, print all names in distinct letters. Neatness is a must.

2. Type on only one side of a standard-sized (8½ by 11) typing paper. Do not use fancy or small note paper. Always double space; leave wide margins.

3. In upper right hand corner put "for immediate release," or "release on **(date)**."

Write your club's name, your name and telephone number in the upper left corner of each page. If there's a question, the editor can phone you. Some editors go so far as to refuse to print unsigned material!

4. Begin about a third of the way down from the top of the first page. This leaves space for the editor to write in the headline or any notations. Don't worry about writing the head; the editor does that.

5. Remember that news columns are narrow. Keep sentences short, usually not more than twenty words. Keep paragraphs to sixty words or less.

6. Most publicity isn't worth more than one typed page. If you feel that cramps your style, write "more" at the bottom of the first page. But—are you sure that extra page is necessary? (Be sure to number each page.)

7. Make carbons of all your stories. These come in handy if the editor wants to check a story over the phone. The carbon copy is also convenient for future reference.

8. Be accurate! Check and double check everything, especially spelling of names. For some reason, we are all a little sensitive about our names! Always give the first name or initials, never just "Mrs. Jones." You should always use the husband's name for a married woman, "Mrs. John Jones," not "Mrs. Mary Jones" unless she is appearing on your program professionally. Avoid nicknames as they look odd in print.

This is certainly no place for a course in journalism, but there are a few general hints to make news-writing easier.

Command attention with that first sentence! The first paragraph is known as your "lead." It should sort of summarize the story, be catchy, and arouse interest. Always lead off with the most important fact about your whole project. That first paragraph helps determine if people will read the rest of the story! Don't be flowery.

(In reverse, don't put essentials into the last paragraph. Much as he might dislike to do it, an editor sometimes must cut a story to fit the space.)

After you get off to a good start, add other facts in order. Don't give your own opinion. Write in the third person—not "I" or "we." Use simple language. Make the story so intriguing you'd like to read it yourself! Your club should sound interesting, friendly, progressive, or fun.

Every story should mention at least one name; three or four are better. Names are news and people like to see their names in print. Hard workers deserve credit.

If local merchants are co-operating, they should be given credit. If an orchestra is playing, by all means give the name.

Include all items, and nothing but the items, that will interest the average reader. Please be brief. You'll get better readership and the editor admires brevity. He has space problems, believe me!

And of course you'll watch your grammar. Don't repeat yourself by saying the same thing two different ways. Avoid unnecessary adjectives.

It's usually helpful to keep in mind the four W's of publicity. They are: What, why, when, where? You can also add the How, if you wish. It's a good idea to answer these briefly in the first paragraph, or lead. The most unusual "W" in your case can lead off. You can vary the order in which you give them, but do not leave any out.

Look for the unusual. Humor might get you a blurb. A newspaper once used an item from a church reporting on a Christmas program. A 3-year-old told her anxiously prompting mother, "Well, Mamma, you just come up here and say it!" It's usually best to address humorous bits to the columnist who uses such type of material.

Try for human interest stories before the event. If you're giving a pet show, use a picture of a cute little girl and her parakeet entry. Or how about a funny incident that happened while putting up bazaar booths?

Give the feature editor a call if you have an unusual factor about the project you're planning. A feature story in a newspaper is grand publicity! Be sure you really have something worthwhile for the write-up.

Photographs

If you're sponsoring an important speaker, or a big name will take part in your project, use his picture. Write or call him for the photo and a brief biography as soon as the date is set. Send this material to the paper as far in advance as possible. Sometimes it takes a week or so to have engravings made. But such news may rate page one!

Never submit pictures in frames; remove them first. Write the name in soft pencil on the back of the picture. Indicate if the picture is to be returned. In addition, type a caption on a slip of paper. Paste it so it extends below the bottom of the picture. Rubber cement usually works best.

Always be sure information and names are absolutely correct on the captions. If several persons are shown, list them "From left to right—"

Submit only high-quality photos, sharp and in focus. They reproduce better if there is marked contrast in light and dark areas, too.

If the affair isn't big enough for the news photographer to cover, get your own. Be sure he is good. Take advance pictures as well as those on the actual day of the event. (If the newspaper can't use the photos, they'll go in a club scrapbook. Or sell prints later to the members for extra profit!)

Check to see what kind and size the paper uses. Most prefer 8 by 10 glossies, but will accept a 5 by 7. A high or "glossy" finish is preferred because it makes the best engraving.

Individual pictures are usually better than group pictures. If you do photograph a group, limit it to only a few. They should be doing something. Informal action pictures always attract more attention than stiff, posed shots. For example, the decorating committee can be actually working on the centerpiece, or whatever.

If you have a small-town weekly, the chances are it can't afford engravings. Here is one solution: your club can offer to pay for having the cut made. Check first to be sure the treasury can stand it. Or the publicity chairman might send the photograph to a daily in a nearby city. She should ask him to send the engraving to the small weekly just as soon as he has published it.

Radio and TV

Study the local radio and television programs. Chances are at least one is the interview type. Ask to have your president, a committee chairman, or a featured performer interviewed before the project takes place.

Radio and TV. Probably there is an interview-type program on a local station. Try to get on it to publicize your event before it takes place.

Radio and TV stations often give spot announcements. Check into it. Write such an item carefully. Be brief. Probably about fifty words are plenty. Begin with a bang and make every word count.

Perhaps the newscaster might mention your project.

Posters

Posters are good publicity—if well done. A few straggly letters on a dirty cardboard won't help your cause much. It may pay you to have the work done professionally. Of course home talent is cheaper and isn't too difficult. Suppose you can't draw or letter. You can still turn out a fairly good poster.

Appearance

A poster must be neat, first of all. It should be easily read. From about how far away will be poster be viewed? The average title (or main words) should be in 2-inch high letters. Add a half inch to each letter for every 15 feet that the viewer stands away from the poster.

Graph paper helps in making a pattern for letters. You can cut out letters and paste them to your show cards.

Amateurs sometimes paste on the letters cut from stiff paper. Then they spray the letters with paint. The paper is peeled off when the paint is dry. You can buy lettering guides if you want to letter direct on the poster.

Pictures enliven a poster. Be as original and clever as possible. Make designs big but keep them simple. You can get dramatic effects with sharp contrasts.

Any pasting should be done with rubber cement. It's easy to remove excess without smudging. You might like to use gummed crepe paper that needs no paste.

There are many materials you can use. Check with an art teacher or at art supply stores for recommended poster materials.

If you're really interested, you might investigate silk screen painting, block prints, stenciling, etc.

Regardless of what type poster you make, there are two musts. It must stop people. Once they've stopped, they must be able to read it!

Information

Use only brief, descriptive words. Detailed information should form a block of copy, with white space around it. Give only essential facts: type of affair, where and when, who is sponsoring it and why (if a special cause). Give price and where tickets may be purchased.

Slant the style, colors, and design to the group you want to attract. Teen-agers, for example, go for a different poster than elderly people.

Placing

Now that you've finished your posters, where do you put them? Principal stores, the post office, other public places. Bulletin boards in churches, schools, and offices are also possibilities. Some cities even allow posters in their buses. BUT ask permission before displaying your posters anywhere.

Other Publicity

In addition to the usual newspaper items, posters, radio and TV announcements, try for novel promotion. There are several ways to call attention to your project.

Beforehand

Mail postal cards or letters to other organizations. If a small town, use the telephone directory, church membership, etc. Letters should be well processed. A typed letter is excellent if your mailing list isn't too long. Multilith, multigraph, or offset all resemble typing more than mimeographing does.

Your lead statement should be startling or ask a question that can be answered with "yes." If you want reservations, enclose a postage-collect reply card.

Postal cards can introduce the affair, or serve as a reminder. Here again you'll want a good sales talk. Cheaper than printing are mimeographing, Cardmaster, Print-o-matic duplicator. If you want a reply, buy double cards.

In writing letters or post cards, think of the persons who'll receive them. Try to sound as if you were writing each, personally.

Circulars or fliers can be distributed. They should be on

colored paper. In addition to the facts, give something to stir up curiosity.

Small boys are usually eager to help distribute them. Give them a small fee or a free ticket.

If circulars are mailed, an 8½ by 11-inch size is convenient. Simply fold it into three folds. Seal the center of the outside with Scotch tape. Address and stamp. Check first with the postal authorities what type circular doesn't have to go first class.

The local theater is a good means of publicity. Inquire how much it costs to flash a notice on the screen.

Don't overlook the possibility of notices in church bulletins and school papers. There may be other booklets in town that might use your items. The Chamber of Commerce may list local events. Some companies have house organs that list activities of interest to their women employees. Such organizations as the YWCA might be helpful in telling others about your activity.

Don't forget the telephone! It gives the personal touch, is next best to dropping in on the person. You'll need a committee to divide the calling list. Serving on this often appeals to the woman who is tied down at home for one reason or another.

The caller should ask first if the person has a few minutes to talk. If not, offer to call back at a more convenient time. Be as brief as possible, even then. Of course you'll be friendly—that goes without saying.

The caller gives the essential details. Try for a definite "yes" or "no" if you want an estimate of attendance. You can even take actual reservations. Or the call could simply serve as a reminder.

Several weeks before the event, post signs all over town. If you can stir up curiosity with them, so much the better. Don't tell all—save that for regular publicity.

The Day

An automobile with a loud speaker is sure to draw attention. Play recorded music, and give the announcement between tunes.

You might put a "sandwich" boy out on the street. Letter two big sheets of cardboard with a brief announcement. Sling these signs fore and aft on a fellow in costume.

Pennants on the street, or even at the place of the project, attract attention. You might go so far as to make hang-tags and buttons to distribute to people. Everybody who wears one advertises your project!

Try to be different. You might paint footprints on the sidewalk leading to your place of "business." Use a stencil. Poster paint or whitewash will wash right off when you are through.

One club who sponsored a white elephant sale used the footprint idea. They painted big "elephant's footprints" leading to their very door!